Steps to the Throne

by
George D. Watson

Author of
Coals of Fire
God's Eagles
Heavenly Life & Types of the Holy Spirit
Holiness Manual & The Seven Overcomeths
Love Abounding
Love and Duty
Our Own God
The Secret of Spiritual Power
Spiritual Feasts
Spiritual Ships
White Robes

SCHMUL PUBLISHING COMPANY
NICHOLASVILLE, KENTUCKY

Cover image copyright: <a href='https://www.123rf.com/profile_archman'>archman / 123RF Stock Photo</a>. Used by permission.

Published by Schmul Publishing Co.
PO Box 776
Nicholasville, KY 40340
USA

Printed in the United States of America

ISBN 10: 0-88019-614-9
ISBN 13: 978-0-88019-614-7

Visit us on the Internet at www.wesleyanbooks.com, or order direct from the publisher by calling 800-772-6657, or by writing to the above address.

Contents

Publisher's Preface

GD WATSON'S UNQUESTIONED HALLMARK was his advocacy of heart holiness. It breathes through his books like a celestial aroma. This book is no exception, although it is ostensibly a book on prophecy. The reader will not get very far into the volume before it becomes apparent that Watson sees a sanctified heart as indispensable to share the Heavenly Throne as promised by Jesus.

Some positions he takes in this book may seem somewhat controversial from the perspective of most readers today, but it should be considered that the study of eschatology was not as fully developed in his day as it is in ours. Even now, honest exegetes often reach very different conclusions in the passages of Revelation and Daniel, and that after more than a century of earnest scriptural study. Watson did not have such an advantage, but forged his way through mostly on his own.

There is no equivocation, however, on the subject of a holy heart. He insists on its absolute necessity for a soul to confidently look forward to the Second Coming and the Millennium. There is nothing murky about that topic in this book.

—D. CURTIS HALE

Publisher, 2018

Preface

FOR TWENTY-FIVE OR THIRTY years of my life I accepted the old Roman Catholic notion, which is accepted by most Protestants, that the second coming of Jesus would be after the millennium [*sic*], and at the time of the general judgment. Then, for a few years, I was unsettled in my views on that subject, for I saw so many portions of Scripture that could not have any reasonable interpretation in harmony with that old theory.

Early in 1896 I began to pray very earnestly for the Holy Spirit to open up the scriptures to me clearly on that subject. In two or three weeks afterward the Spirit began unfolding to my mind, in a remarkable way, the Book of Revelation, and the parables of Jesus, and other scriptures on the pre-millennial coming of Christ, and the light on that subject has been increasing ever since. Some years ago I published a small book, called "The Seven Overcomeths," giving only the interpretation that applied to the interior spiritual life, but did not then see their ulterior and perfect relation to the coming of Jesus, and His millennial reign. I have given in this book what the Spirit has given to me of the application of the seven overcomeths, not only to the inner life in the present state, but their application as preparing the believer to reign with Jesus in His coming kingdom.

If my life is spared, I have several other books to write upon this subject. I trust the blessed Comforter will apply the things in the following pages to the hearts of many thousands, and stir God's children to prepare themselves to meet the coming King.

—G.D.W.

Denver, Col., April 30, 1898

Chapter I
THE EMBLEMS IN REVELATION

IT OFTEN HAPPENS THAT when the head of a great government wishes to communicate very secret and important matter to one of its ministers in a foreign land it adopts a cipher code, that is a language in signs, so as to transmit the message without any one being able to understand it, except the person to whom it is sent. This is precisely what Jesus did in the Book of Revelation. We are told that God gave this revelation to his Son Jesus, and Jesus gave it in signs, or telegraphic ciphers, to an angel, and the angel gave these signs unto John. Hence this last and crowning book of God's word, is written out largely in ciphers. This was done in order that the message might be safely transmitted through the dark ages. If the Romanists had perfectly understood in centuries gone by, all the teachings of this book, they would have destroyed it from the earth; and so God adopted a method of sign language, in order that no one might understand it except those for whom it was especially designed. As the coming of Christ gets nearer, the Holy Spirit is more and more revealing the secrets of this wonderful book to His humble and thoughtful servants in all the earth; and many things which have been concealed through the Dark Ages are now beginning to be unfolded in the clear light, which the Holy Spirit is pouring upon those who are entirely devoted to God. Let us remember, that the Holy Spirit selects His emblems with a perfect scientific accuracy, and all the metaphors and symbols used in Scripture are chosen with infallible wisdom. If we take the pains to read the Book of Revelation, and cull out all the various emblems which are used therein, we will find that all of them are explained in the book itself. And if we can discover the meaning of these various types we have the secret key to unlock nearly everything in the book. It is my purpose in this volume to give an exegesis of the second, third and fourth chapters, showing more particularly the connection between Christian holiness and the coming reign of Jesus on this earth; but I have thought it well to give in this chapter a brief explanation of the various emblems in the book, that the common reader may be able to pursue an individual study of all the book.

"Stars" in this book represent Ministers, more particularly the office of the Minister, not only a church Minister, but also a State Minister. Hence it denotes Princes, or under rulers in Church or State.

"Candlesticks" represent separate congregations of Christians, not a denomination, or a great body, but simply congregations, or a church in its local and social organic form.

"Heaven" in this book, in the majority of instances, means God's Kingdom among men. This will be kept strictly in view, for all sorts of erroneous and fantastic interpretations of this book have resulted from the notion that the word "Heaven" means the third Heavens where God the Father has His throne of glory. The word "Heaven" as used in the parables of Jesus, refers continually to God's Kingdom among men, and, in nearly every instance, this word Heaven is in the Greek in the plural number, proving that it is a term of large and manifold meaning. Jesus says: "The Kingdom of the Heavens is like a net cast into the sea, in which were gathered both good fish and bad fish," which simply means the Kingdom of God on this earth. In like manner the word Heaven, in most places in Revelation, means the Kingdom of God among men, and when we read, "I saw a great sign in Heaven," that is in the Kingdom of God on earth. And again, "there was war in Heaven," which refers emphatically to the great Reformation of Martin Luther, and the conflict between the Protestants and the Catholics. The old notion that there was war in the third Heavens, where the Father has His throne, is a teaching of Catholicism and the dream of poets, but utterly unscriptural. No war has ever agitated those bright regions of eternal glory.

"Woman" in this book, is always a type of an organized body of professed Christians. Throughout the entire Bible, woman is a type of the church, and, when used in the plural number, represents the various branches and organized bodies of professed worshipers of God. If this type were always remembered it would save the reader from a great many foolish interpretations of this book. For instance, those who are spoken of in Chapter 14 as the Bride of the Lamb, are said to be "pure virgins," "who were not defiled with other women." The word "women" means the various branches, and bodies of ecclesiastical systems, which become worldly, and fashionable, and filled up with various carnal practices. But those believers who are sanctified, and wedded to Christ, are delivered from all ecclesiastical corruption. And the picture is that of *one* pure woman, keeping herself from the various carnal practices of other women, that is of other organized church bodies.

"Sun" in this book, typifies a King, or a Kingdom, that is royal splendor, imperial power. And in many other portions of Scripture, the word "sun" represents kingly authority. When Joseph in his dream saw the sun, moon, and stars bow to him, the sun was a type of Jacob, who was really a King, the moon a type of his mother, who was a Queen, and the stars, a type of his brethren, who were Princes and Ministers of State. Hence, throughout this book, the "sun" means kingly authority, as when John saw the "woman," that is the Christian Church, "clothed with the sun," that is imperial splendor. Again, the angel standing in the sun, to proclaim war, represents the angel of God, stirring up all the royal heads among the nations to declare war.

"Moon" typifies a Queen, or a minor King, or Principality, a sub-King. As when "the woman clothed with the sun," had the moon under her foot, that is the great Catholic church, clothed in royalty, had all the other Kings and Queens and Princes of the Christian world, under her foot, which was literally the case for 1000 years.

"Four beasts" in Revelation, should always be read "four living creatures." The word "four beasts" is a horrible translation of the original, which is the very word used for eternal life. So always read the "four living creatures," which are the same creatures described by Ezekiel, and Isaiah, as the seraphim and cherubim. They always represent glorified saints, especially those who take high rank in the Kingdom of grace and glory. Hence these "four living creatures," are represented as being in the throne with Jesus, during His millennial reign. They certainly are saved and glorified men, for in one place we are told, that they praise God for having been saved and washed in Christ's blood from among the nations. "Beasts," when not connected with the word "four," always represents human governments, and especially professedly Christian governments, which are yet full of tyranny, and oppression, political scheming, and selfishness, and greed. The Greek word for "beast" in all such places, is a very different word from the four living creatures, and signifies a wild, bloodthirsty beast of the forest, a true type of the ambition, and greed, and tyranny of politicians.

"Smoke" in this book, represents whatever comes out of the mouth, in the form of either prayer, or blasphemy. Prayer is represented by incense, a sweet, fragrant smoke, typifying the fragrance of the prayers of God's servants. But blasphemy and cursing from the mouths of those who are lost, are represented by the smoke of burning sulphur.

"Fowls" in this book, is always an emblem of demons, and evil spirits. In fact this is the type of the fowls of the air, all through the Bible. Jesus says, "the fowls of the air picked up the grain that had been sown by the wayside," and afterwards tells us these fowls are devils. In His parable on the Christian church, he represents it as a mustard plant, growing so large that the fowls of the air lodged in its branches, which has been sadly fulfilled, in the fact that myriads of demons lodge in the various branches of the nominal church. Hence the "fowls" that fatten on the horses, and on captains, and on warriors, represent the demons feasting themselves on a battlefield, for they delight in the slaughter of human beings.

"Waters" represent the souls of mankind. Hence the woman sitting on many waters, represents the organized church of Rome, presiding over the souls of many nations. Muddy water represents wicked souls, casting up mire and dirt. Clear, glassy water, represents pure souls, cleansed from all sinful tempers and desires, and filled with a beautiful transparency, without guile, without evil tempers, like unto clear glass. This is the picture of what the souls of men will be in the millennial age, when they will be presided over by the glorified saints of the Bridehood, who are represented as standing upon the glassy sea.

"Man-child" in this book, is a type of the martyrs, who were slain by the Romish church during the Dark Ages. It is a great mistake to call the "man-child" in chapter 12 Jesus, for the prophecy in that chapter refers emphatically to something that had not occurred at the time John was alive. The "man-child" represents those Protestants who were converted and sanctified inside the bosom of the Romish church, and which caused her trouble and sorrow.

"Red dragon" is a type of the Romish Inquisition. It was the incarnation of the devil, in an organized institution for bloody murder, to capture and kill the Protestants, as soon as they dared confess their saving faith. Hence the "Red dragon stood in front of the woman," that is in front of the church, to devour her children, that is to slay the Protestants, as quick as they were born, that is, as soon as they confessed their faith.

"Horses" in this book represent organized aggression. In all ages the horse is a type of organized and swift power. The horse is the swiftest of all animals, and the one mostly used in times of war. The word "horse" is used among all nations in Proverbs, as "war-horse," and "swift as a race-horse," and such expressions.

The "white horse" represents organized and aggressive holiness, pushing its way from pentecost out among the nations.

The "red horse'" represents organized opposition to Jesus, and bloody wars against the truth.

The "black horse'" represents organized ignorance, darkness, superstition, such as was the case in the Dark Ages.

The "pale horse'" represents organized forms of ecclesiastical back-sliding, where bodies of believers, professing to be alive, have a pale and ghastly type of life, such as is the case at the present day.

"Winds" represent heresies, terrible delusions, terrific scourgings from God, the great tribulations, which are to be let loose on the earth, just as soon as God gets all His elect Bride wholly sanctified, and sealed with the baptism of the Holy Ghost and fire.

"Vials'" represent the outpouring of God's wrath and judgment upon different nations, and at different periods, such as the French Revolution, and the late Civil War in America, and similar events.

"Frogs" represent evil spirits, going forth to seduce the people into false systems of faith. These frogs take on the form of spiritualism, Swedenborgianism, Christian science, theosophy, Mormonism, and baal-worship in the various lodges of secret societies.

A "pure river" represents the Holy Spirit, which flows out eternally from the Father and from the Son.

The "Tree of Life" represents Jesus, as the incarnate Redeemer and Savior.

The number 144,000 represents that elect company through all the ages, who have measured up to a life of perfect faith and obedience, and who have been qualified to form the Bride of the Lamb. This number is used because it is a multiple of 12, for the number 12 in Scripture always represents the Kingdom of God.

Three represents the Trinity, Father, Son, and Holy Ghost.

Four represents humanity, especially redeemed and glorified humanity.

Six represents imperfection, the number by which Satan counterfeits the work of God.

Seven represents salvation, or the Christ life in His saints, for as 3 and 4 make 7, so God and man, united, constitute salvation.

Ten represents the number for multitude, as thousands, or tens of thousands, etc.

Twelve represents the Divine government, for as 3 times 4 make 12, so God multiplies himself in His creatures, which constitutes His government.

Forty represents proving, testing, trying.

Fifty is the complete cycle number, the jubilee number, hence a type of the Millennial Kingdom, when creation will be restored to its normal condition.

There are a few other emblems, which are used, which I may refer to in succeeding chapters. But if these types are kept in mind, the ordinary reader will be able to have a common sense and satisfactory understanding of the knowledge of the things that God has been pleased to make known to us in this wonderful and last book of His infallible word.

Chapter II
"THE SEVEN CHURCHES"
Rev. 1:11

IN ORDER TO ARRIVE AT any correct understanding of these three chapters, which we have laid before us for our study in this book, we must endeavor to find out the significance of these seven churches, which Christ selected, to whom the message of the apocalyptic visions were especially sent. The Bible is God's sample book. The Holy Spirit could doubtless have given us thousands of Bibles similar to the one we have, and all of them been filled with remarkable characters and incidents, but He has selected samples of men, and events, and truths, which His wisdom saw were best adapted for our instruction and salvation. From the hundreds of churches which existed in the days of St. John. Jesus selected these seven churches of Asia, with a view of setting forth the various stages of the Christian churches, from the days of John until the coming of Jesus, and the close of the Gentile Age. We see in these seven churches, samples of all the Christian churches of all the Ages. There is not a congregation of professed Christians in the world, which perhaps is not in the condition of one of these seven churches. So that in whatever stage a church may be, either in its holiness or corruption, it will find itself actually mirrored in the looking-glass of the second and third chapters of Revelation. This same truth applies with equal force to all individual members of the church. Every separate member of the Christian church will find himself represented in one of these various congregations. It is a melancholy reflection, that out of these seven churches there are only two which escape condemnation, or a reproof from the Lord. From this we learn that a small minority, either of separate congregations, or of individual members, are living in such union with Jesus as to have His perfect approbation. But the main lesson to be drawn from these seven churches is, that here we see set forth the various stages of the Christian church, from the days of the apostles until Christ's second coming.

"The Church of Ephesus" represents the Christians in the first century. They are described as "having abundant works, and patience, and orthodoxy, and they tried those who professed to be apostles, and were not, and they had many extra-ordinary virtues, yet Jesus said they had left their first love." This word, "first love," must not be understood to mean the love of a young convert, but it was first love in the point of rank and quality. God wants our love, pure and tender, and warm, and personal, over and above all other things, or labors, or sacrifices and nothing grieves the Infinite heart more quickly than to see our personal affection for Him is cooling down. This was the condition of the Christian church, even before the death, or the translation of, St. John, as many suppose he was translated to Heaven,

"The Church of Smyrna'" represents the condition of

Christian believers in the second and third centuries, during the great persecutions from the heathen. Jesus told this church that the devil would cast them into prison, that they should be tried, and have tribulation ten days, and for them not to be afraid of the things they should suffer, and though they had outward poverty, yet in grace they were rich, and that if they were faithful unto death, he would give them a crown of life. During the second and third centuries the Roman Emperor issued edicts of persecution against the Christians, and there were ten of these great imperial persecutions, which was the fulfillment of the "ten days tribulation" prophesied of them. In those persecutions, Christians were frequently covered with tar, and oil, and set on fire at night, to make bonfires for the thousands of heathen Romans to look upon with fiendish delight. At other times they were thrown into an arena of wild beasts, and torn to pieces, while the great amphitheater was filled with people, who shouted and laughed, to see the wild beasts devouring Christians. These persecutions kept the church pure, hence we find there is not a word of reproof for the church of Smyrna, but everything of encouragement and approbation.

"The Church of Pergamos" represents what the Christian church was in the fourth and fifth centuries. In this church we find a mixedness, some were very spiritual, being faithful even to martyrdom, but others were stumbling blocks, and holding on to false and ruinous doctrines, especially the doctrine of the Nicolaitanes, "which held that the body could commit sin, and be full of iniquity, while the soul could remain pure." This was the Age in which the Emperor Constantine professed the Christian faith, and reversed all the edicts of persecution, and began to shower favors upon the church, and load the Bishops and Christian Ministers, with many emoluments and gifts. This was the beginning of the downfall of spiritual Christianity, and the beginning of the formation of all the Christian societies into one great ecclesiastical system, which became the Roman Catholic Church. Up to this time, the churches were not formed into one organic body of church government, and from this time the love of many waxed cold, and many erroneous doctrines began to creep into the Christian ministry, and there began that horrible amalgamation of heathen philosophy with Christian doctrine. Hence the Romish Church is a conglomerate mass, in which Judaism, and heathenism, and Christianity, are all merged into one system.

"The Church of Thyatira" represents what the church was from the sixth to the twelfth centuries. Thyatira was a wealthy, fashionable city, and silk emporium, and therefore is used to symbolize the worldly and fashionable splendor of backslidden Christianity. There was in the church at Thyatira, a woman preacher named Jezebel, who taught and practiced the doctrine of free love. Jesus selected this woman, and her teaching and practice, to represent what the Romish Church was during the Dark Ages. It was during these centuries, that the Christian Church became united with the State government, which has always been an abomination to the Lord, and is denounced as spiritual fornication. When the Roman Empire was destroyed by the invasion of the Goths and Vandals from the north of Europe, the Caesars were dethroned. Then the Bishops and Rulers of the Christian Church, obtained the ascendency in the politics of Europe, and the church became the dominant power over all State rulers. It was then that Popery was instituted, and it was recognized as the ruler of the world. John saw in his vision, "a woman sitting upon a beast." The "woman" represents the Roman Catholic Church, and the "beast" represents the Roman Empire, hence the church governed the politics and Kingdoms of what was former the Roman Empire. This was the period which Ave dominate the Dark Ages.

"The Church of Sardis" typifies the period from the thirteenth to the fifteenth centuries, just before the Great Reformation in Germany and England. Of this church Christ says, thou hast a name that thou livest, and art dead. He also says, thou hast a few names even in Sardis, which have not defiled their garments. These few undefiled ones represent those holy persons that arose in the church during that period, as burning and shining lights of perfect love, such as Thomas a Kempis, and John Thaller, and John of the Cross, and many saintly persons, whose writings on spirituality became the seed of the Reformation. It was during these centuries that there came what is called the Revival of Letters. Printing was invented, and many began to study the laws of nature, and poetry, and works on philosophy and science began to be published.

"The Church of Philadelphia" covers the period of the Reformation. This revolt from the darkness and superstition of Romanism began simultaneously in France, and Germany, and England, and covered a period of about 200 years, from the fifteenth to the seventeenth centuries. This Reformation embraces the great work of Martin Luther, and his coadjutors in Germany, and the Revival in France under the Huguenots, and in England under Ridley and Wycliff, and a little later under George Fox, the founder of the Quaker society, and broke out afresh a century later, under the Great Wesleyan Revival. All the modern churches of Protestantism had their origin in these Great Reformations, and every one of them began in a revival of Scriptural holiness. These various churches of the Reformation were not under the same church government, but were bound together in a spirit of Christian fraternity. The word "Philadelphia" means "brotherly love," and hence the church in that city was chosen to represent the churches of the Reformation. Against this church there is no condemnation, but Jesus says "He set before it an open door which no man could shut." God providentially opened up to the churches of the Reformation, all of England, and Germany, and the Western world, which was a fulfillment of the words, "I have set before thee an open door." At the close of the message to the Church of Philadelphia, Jesus says, "Behold I come quickly, see that no man take thy crown." Here is an intimation, that from the time of the churches of the Reformation, the coming of the Lord would begin to be manifested to his servants, and warning the church of that period to hold fast to the liberty and holiness to which it had attained, that it might be prepared to be glorified with Christ, and with Him wear the crown of dominion through the Millennial Age.

"The Church of Laodicea" covers the period of the backsliding of all the Protestant churches, down to the time when Christ shall appear to glorify the saints, and institute His reign on earth. We are now living in this period, which proves that the end of this Age is nearly finished. Jesus says of the church of this period, "I know thy works, that thou art neither cold nor hot." That is, the churches are full of various kinds of works, but the works are partly spiritual, and partly political, and partly scientific, and partly of a mere social character, so that the whole is characterized by lukewarmness. The church of this period, boasts that she is rich, and increased with goods, and has need of nothing, which is exactly the case in the various denominations of churches at the present time. They build fine structures, and great universities, and have great ecclesiastical gatherings, and complicated church machinery, and boast of their learning, and culture, and science, and art, and eloquence, and music, and statistics, and are intoxicated with the dream that they are going to conquer the world, and thereby bring the millennium, without the personal and visible presence of Jesus. But amid all this boasting the Infinite Searcher of hearts declares that these churches are wretched, and miserable, and poor, and blind, and naked. They are destitute of real heart sanctification, humility of mind, and personal affection for God, and the blessed indwelling of the personal Holy Ghost, they deny the supernatural in the pentecostal displays of saving power, do not believe in deep emotional religion, or in remarkable manifestations, or in divine healing, or in those heavenly corruscations of spiritual fire, and love, that characterized the Church of Pentecost, and the early days of reformation. It is of this church, that Jesus says, "I am about to vomit them out of my mouth." (See Greek.) It is in this period of the Laodicean church, that God has started the great movement of Christian holiness, which has swept for 25 or 30 years through the churches of Christendom, and this movement of sanctification is the hand of God, knocking at the door of all these modern churches, and appealing to their individual members, that if any one of them will open the door, Christ will enter in and cleanse and fill such an one, and sup with him preliminary to the Marriage Supper of the Lamb, which is soon to transpire, when He gathers out His elect saints at His appearing. This is the closing message to all the churches of the present Gentile Age.

In the following chapters, let us go back and review the various promises made to these churches, and see what are the qualifications, and the steps of spiritual victory, requisite for obtaining a place at the table of the Marriage Supper, and a place in the government of the Millennial Kingdom.

Chapter III
"HEAR WHAT THE SPIRIT SAITH"
Rev. 2:7

AMONG THE VERY FIRST conditions of being qualified for membership in the Bridehood of Jesus is that of having a willing and obedient heart to hear voice of the Holy Spirit. Seven times within the limits of the second and third chapters of Revelation, Jesus commands us to hear what the Spirit shall say. Our Savior tells us that nobody can come to the Son of God, except the Father shall draw him. It is the office of the Father, through the operation of His law applied by the Spirit, to awaken us and draw us in the spirit of repentance, to go to Jesus for pardon and renewal of life. Then when Jesus receives us, and remits our sins, and gives us power to become sons of God. He then leads us to the personality and fullness of the Holy Spirit. He tells us to tarry until we are endued with power from on high, and that He will pray the Father, and we shall receive another Comforter, which is the Holy Ghost, who will sanctify us through the truth, and take the things of Christ, and reveal them unto us. When it is said, the Lord is my Shepherd, and He leadeth me beside the still waters, it is simply a picture of Jesus, after saving us from our sins, leading us to the clear river of the ever-flowing Holy Spirit, that we may be filled with pure love, and put under the dominion of the abiding Comforter. Then, when the Holy Spirit gets possession of our nature and life, He in turn leads us back to the eternal Father, and reveals to us in ever-widening and brightening fields of light, the personalities, and love, paid fellowship, of the Father and the Son. The Father leads us to the Son, and the Son leads us to the Holy Spirit, and the Holy Spirit leads us back to the uncreated and unbegotten person of the Father, from whom eternally comes the Son, and from whom eternally proceeds the Holy Spirit. This is the beautiful, fascinating circuit, around which the re-deemed soul travels, with ever-increasing light and love.

1. In order to hear what the Spirit saith, we must have ears that are Spiritual, to know His voice. Man has a body, Greek *soma*, and a soul, Greek *psyche*, from which we get the word "psychological," and then he has a spirit, Greek *pneuma*. A failure to recognize this threefold nature of man, has been the cause of a thousand blunders in religious teaching and experience.

The great mass of professed Christians simply regard man in his twofold nature, of body and soul, and thereby confound the reasoning faculties, with man's moral and spiritual being, and hence regard the Christian religion as a mere system of doctrines, and opinions, and creeds, and that religious experience is merely on the plain of the natural, mental faculties, a mere thing of sentiment and psychology. The Scriptures abundantly teach us, that there is an "inner man" of the spiritual nature, and that this "inner man" has spiritual senses of hearing, seeing, touching, tasting, and smelling, and is endowed with spiritual intuitions, and instincts, which are just as definite and real as those which the body has in connection with the nervous and mental system. In the case of the natural man, this spiritual nature is utterly dormant, the inner senses are there, but closed in a state of sleep. There are certain animals that hibernate during the winter, or lie frozen for months in the ground, and are utterly unconscious of life or sensation. But in the spring they thaw out, and their senses are brought to life by the warm sun, then they can see and hear and move. In like manner the spirit of a sinner is in a state of moral death, as if frozen, but under the warm light of repentance, and saving faith, and the new birth, these inner spiritual faculties are open to consciousness, and the play of divine things upon them. Then, under the sanctifying power of the Holy Spirit, these senses of the inner spirit are purified, and intensified, and enlarged, so that they can detect the sights, and sounds, and sweetness, and beauty, and realty of spiritual things, of divine truth, and divine personalities, and heavenly experiences. This is why our Lord says so often, "He that hath ears to hear let him hear."

2. Unless we have this threefold nature of man in mind, and clearly recognize the realm of the inner spirit, as being that part of our nature, upon which the Holy Ghost operates in a direct manner, producing supernatural and heavenly experiences, we will never understand the full teachings of Scripture, or the real sphere of the spiritual life. The soul is that part of our nature which looks out through the body, toward the realm of nature, through the bodily senses, with its reason, comparison, and natural affections, and sentiments, and emotions. Our inner spirit opens out toward God, and toward the whole supernatural world. There are two words for "love" in the Greek Testament, one is *philia*, which always means human love, and should have been translated uniformly by

our word "affection. The other word is in the Greek *agape,* which invariably means divine love. Now the word *philia,* or human affection, has its seat in the soul, in the mental nature, but the word *agape,* divine love, has its seat in the inner spirit. Hence those two words in their uses in the Greek Testament, mark the distinction between man's soulish nature, and spiritual nature. Now there are myriads of professed Christians, who have never had their spiritual nature thoroughly aroused, and renewed, but who have a mental religion, and love God merely in their human, soulish *philia,* or human affection. Thousands on thousands in the church, love God just about like they love the founders of their country, or as they love their political parties, or their earthly friends. Such persons are not saved, and it is exceedingly difficult to get them to see the need of a divine, supernatural salvation. This truth is forcibly manifested in the conversation which James had with Peter, just before our Savior's ascension. After restoring the disciples to Himself, after His resurrection, Jesus said to Peter, who claimed to love Christ more than anybody else, "Simon, do you have divine love for me?" (Greek Agape.) Peter said. "Thou knowest I have human affection for you." (Greek Philia.) The second time, Jesus said. "Have you divine love for me?" and the second time, Peter said, "I have human affection for you." And then the third time, Jesus dropped down to the level of Peter's human love, and said. "Do you really have human affection for me?" and this pierced Peter's heart to the core. But after pentecost, Peter rose to the level of Christ's spiritual love, and used the word *agape,* divine love, ever after. Now in order for us to hear what the Spirit saith, we must be spiritual beings, with our spiritual nature vitalized, and illuminated, so that we can recognize things in the spiritual world, just as readily and vividly, as our inward senses recognize the phenomena of the material world.

3. When our inward spirits are thoroughly purified, and filled with the indwelling Comforter, it becomes by far the dominant and controlling part of our compound being. Persons who live on the plane of the animal nature, regard the body and its senses as all-powerful. But persons who have their soulish nature enlarged, and exercised, and their minds greatly illuminated, and educated, come to realize that the mind is greater than the body. But when the spirit is thoroughly purified, and supernaturalized by the great floods of pure love, and divine light, it arises to an altitude of strength, and dominion, over all the reasoning faculties, and the bodily senses. It is in this condition, that the imagination and reasoning and propensities of the mind and the body, are brought in subjection to that lofty, and serene Christ-life, which is spoken of by the apostle.

4. The Holy Spirit who made the voice, and made language, can most certainly utter Himself in the inner being of His own children, in such a way as to be clearly understood. The inner spirit of man is the region of intuition, and the birthplace of axiomatic truisms. As the body has its appetites, and senses, and as the mind has its reasoning, so the spirit has its intuition, and instinctive perception of divine verities. Hence the Holy Spirit speaks to us through the channel of these intuitions, which always act instantaneously, and independent of our surroundings, and superior to logic. The Spirit often speaks to us by inward mental voices, distinctly recognized by the spiritual ear, and this voice may be at times, so penetrating, and distinct, that it seems an audible voice uttered through the air upon the outward ear, as in the case of young Samuel. The Holy Spirit may again speak to us, by vision, that is by flashing upon the inward retina of our spirit, a beautiful vista of light, or open up spiritual scenery, and spiritual events, to

the interior eye of the mind, which are oftentimes more indelibly fastened upon us than any scene in nature. He may also speak to us through dreams. If we belong to God, we are just as much His when we are asleep as when we are awake, and in all generations the Holy Spirit has spoken to His servants in the dreams of night, and when He so speaks, there is something so peculiar and extraordinary in it, that the believer never confounds such dreams with the ordinary vagaries of a lawless imagination. At other times He speaks to us through His word, by directing to some special passage, or marvelously lighting up some obscurity in the Scriptures, or revealing whole trains of new truth. Again He speaks to us through our love nature, drawing us out after God, with intense yearnings and sweet attractions towards the things He wants us to know. Again He speaks to us by giving extraordinary discernment into the movements of Providence, and causing us to see through the network of His government in the affairs of men as through a thin veil. The ignoring of the voice of the Holy Spirit is the bane of modern Christianity, which has fallen below the plane of the supernatural, and recognizes nothing but the laws of nature, by which is meant the physical world, and the processes of carnal reason.

5. Many think it is dangerous to get into a spiritual realm, where we can hear the voice of God and become familiar with supernatural phenomena in the life of the soul. But the danger lies in a fictitious religion, which is open to all the devices of Satan. It is always dangerous to run a ship in shallow water, and real safety lies in going out to sea. So with the spiritual life, the danger lies in a lack of the Holy Spirit. The blessed Holy Ghost is as safe a guide as is the eternal Father, or the lowly Jesus, and it must grieve His infinite loving nature that myriads of professed Christians

are afraid of Him, and will not dare trust themselves to His full possession. The Holy Spirit in all the manifold operations within us, will never do a thing that contradicts the revealed word of God, or that clashes with a manifest Divine Providence. God cannot antagonize Himself, and the inner and the outer movements of His will are always found to harmonize. It is the reality of the abiding Holy Spirit within us, bringing us into conscious communion with the three persons of the one ever-blessed God, and speaking to us through His many-languaged dialect, that gives real supernatural power to our lives, and puts into our work a divine force, and makes us in many instances an incomprehensible enigma to carnal people, just because He is making us more beautifully intelligible to that innumerable company of angels, and the spirits of just men made perfect, and the church of the first born, into whose blessed fellowship we are brought by the Spirit of glory and of God which abides in us.

Chapter IV
"Eat of the Tree of Life"

Rev. 2:7

To each of the seven churches Jesus makes a special promise if they will overcome. These special promises are doubtless given with an infinite fitness of wisdom, in connection with the several churches, and also in connection with the true, victorious believers, in the several stages of Christianity, set forth by the seven churches. But in all correct interpretations of Scripture we must re-member that it always has more than one fulfillment. The same Scripture has one fulfillment in the individual, and another in the collective body of believers. It has one fulfillment in the inner, spiritual life, and another in the outward, visible, and providential history. It has one fulfill- ment in the present Age, and another in the coming Age of glorification. Hence to confine any one scripture to a single application will lead to much error and misunderstanding of many portions of God's word. This is what the apostle means, when he says "no scripture is of any private interpretation," that is, it must not be confined to one single application, as only to one person, or one place. Thus while these several promises, given to the seven churches, had a fitness to those churches as they then existed in Asia, the same promises have had a special fitness to the real overcoming believers in the various seven stages of the history of the church, and furthermore they have a beautiful and close fitting application to the various steps of the individual believer, as he progresses from the new birth through all the degrees of Christian life, till he reaches his place in the Millennial Kingdom with Jesus. We shall find a regular consecutive order in these promises, which resemble the steps up to a throne. The first of these promises involves the impartation of the divine life to the believer. To him that will hear what the Spirit saith, and overcome his sins, Jesus says, "I will give him to eat of the tree of life, which is in the midst of the Paradise of God." Various truths which grow out of this promise may be arranged as follows:

1. God cannot bless *nothing*. He must have some living being upon whom to confer His blessings. Hence, throughout all Scripture, the impartation of life is the fundamental work of God, both in creation and redemption. Before the Creator could bless Adam, or confer upon him the rights of dominion, He must "breathe into his nostrils the breath of life, and make him a living soul." In the twelvefold blessing that Moses promised upon the tribes of Israel, the first one was the blessing of life. He said, "Let Reuben live," and from that fundamental blessing of life, all the other twelve blessings are arranged, in a consecutive order of ascending blessings, arising to a climax. The same thing is true of these seven overcomeths, which begins by eating the tree of life, and proceeds in a beautiful ascending climax of promise and blessing, un-

til the victorious believer is glorified, and sits with his Lord in the Millennial Throne.

2. The life that Jesus imparts to the soul in regeneration is emphatically a divine life, and yet it is in some mysterious sense a different species of life from that which the angels and other holy and intelligent beings of other worlds may have. There is nothing more marvelous and bewildering in all the universe than life, and then the almost infinite variety of life. There are seven different types, or grades of life, cognizable to our thought. The lowest is mineral life, for the very rocks grow, and have a life which we cannot search out. Then comes infusorial life, which doubtless embraces numberless species, and covers that territory that lies between minerals and vegetables. Then comes vegetable life, which fills an enormous region in nature, extending from microscopical plants, and mosses, up to the gigantic trees of California, hundreds of feet high, and thousands of years old. The different species of vegetable life have perhaps never yet been numbered. Next comes the great world of animal life, extending from insects so small that the natural vision can not see them, to the great elephant, and whale varieties. Next comes the mental, or what the Greeks would call, the soulish life. This takes in the natural feelings, passions, and affections of the human soul, apart from divine grace. And away above these is the life of grace, the divine life, through Jesus imparted to the immortal Spirit in the new birth, by which we become sons of God, being born from above, born of the Holy Spirit. And then, towering above this in altitude far out of sight, is the life of glorification, which is so powerful that it swallows up death in victory. Now we see that between each of these Kingdoms of life, there are great and impassable gulfs, across which no development, or evolution, or mingling of species, can possibly construct a bridge. The fiat of God holds true with regard to each Kingdom of life, namely, that which

is born of the flesh is flesh, and that which is born of the
Spirit is spirit, This divine decree is an impassable wall
between each Kingdom of life, which cannot be climbed
over. That which is born of vegetable is vegetable, that
which is born of animal is animal, that which is born of
the Holy Spirit is spiritual, and that which is born into a
glorified realm is glorified. Hence it is eternally impossible for the natural life of the soul, to develop into a spiritual life, without the intervention of a supernatural and
Heavenly birth. Now as there are hundreds of different
species of life in the same life kingdom, such as the vary-
ing species of vegetable and of animal life, so it is very
evident there are many species of spiritual life, and when
a sinner is pardoned and regenerated through the virtue
of the death of Jesus, and by the Holy Ghost, it is certain
he receives into his spirit a divine life, and yet it is not the
exact form or variety of spiritual life that an unfallen angel possesses. It may be, and likely is, a higher species of
divine life, than that of the angels, because it is transmitted through the incarnation and sacrifice of the second
person in the Godhead. It is not only a divine life, but a
divine life which comes through the incarnation of a divine person. Every type of life is a fathomless mystery,
and can never be searched out by science. In making ex-
periments upon vital protoplasm, through the finest mi-
croscopes, it is impossible to detect in the earliest stages
of any living thing, the difference between one creature
and another. The vital substance, or protoplasm, of a bird,
or worm, or vegetable, or four-footed animal, or a human being, in the earliest inception of its existence, all
look alike. And yet there is in each of these creatures, an
invisible potency, which no human eye can discover, but
which differentiates each life from the other, and as the
life grows, it shows to what kingdom it belongs. When
the Holy Ghost regenerates a penitent believer, he depos-
its divine truth and love and life into the immortal spirit

of the man, and as that life grows, and takes on volume, and force, if the hindrances of that life are purged away, and it is properly nourished, it will infallibly show itself to be like the man Christ Jesus, with as much certainty as the life germ of an eagle, or a lamb, will come to the estate of the eagle or the lamb.

3. The term Tree of Life is very significant. Any tree is a divine poem, a marvelous creation of wisdom, which no mind of man has yet fathomed. A fruit tree is an exquisite and intricate type of the Lord Jesus. There lie hid away in the bosom of the earth, inexhaustible resources of chemical juices, sufficient to feed millions of population. But how can we get that ocean of unseen juices out of the earth, converted into fruit for the sustenance of these hungry millions? A fruit tree is God's invention to mediate between earth's juices and the mouths of the hungry multitudes. The tree spreads its roots out, deep and broad, in the soil, and gathers up, with mysterious energy, the heat and light of the sun, the sugar, and starch, and other nourishing substances, and gases, from the earth, the rain, and the air, and through its trunk and by its sap, transmutes all these into blossom, and delicious fruit, and the multitudes are fed. The earth in this case represents the infinite and eternal substance of the three persons in the Godhead, and the incarnation of the eternal Son, in a human Body, and a human Soul, coming forth in our world, is like that tree. He draws up into His precious body the attributes and qualities of the infinite divinity, and transmutes them into a form of life, which by faith we can eat of, and be nourished thereby in our spirits, just as really as our bodies feed on the fruit, which the tree has brought to us out of the unseen storehouses of the earth. The humanity of Jesus is the trunk of the tree, through which we receive divine love, and perhaps we shall see in eternity, as we cannot now, that we get a higher measure and sweeter form of divine love, through

the humanity of the Son of God, than could possibly have been transmitted to us in any other manner.

4. This promise will doubtless have its ultimate fulfillment in the glorified state. There may be literal trees of life in the Paradise of God, upon whose fruit glorified creatures live. There is nothing in the word of God, or the analogies of Christian reason, to contradict such a conclusion. And we will have occasion to revert to this again farther on in this book. But if such is the case, they will still be but blessed visible emblems of that divine nourishment, that eternal banquet, which will be furnished to our immortal spirits, through the glorified humanity of Jesus. What a joy it is for any created thing to live, and every living thing has a mysterious pleasure in its life. But the joy of living the Christ life, must surpass all others. To love with the same love that Jesus had, to think over His thoughts, to feel with His sympathies, to share the interior instincts of His heart, to pray out of the breath of His prayers, to grow with His growth, and to know in the light of His knowledge, this is the glorious calling that God offers to penitent sinners, this is to eat of the tree of life.

Chapter V
"Not Hurt of the Second Death"
Rev. 2:11

THE NEXT STEP in the qualification for obtaining a place of royalty with Jesus, is that of so overcoming by faith of all the difficulties in the way of Christian growth, as not to be hurt of the second death. In order to understand what the second death is, we must have a scriptural knowledge of what is the first death. When God told Adam that in the day he ate of the fruit of the tree of good and evil, he should surely die; the literal rendering would be, "in dying, thou shalt surely die." That is in the day he ate of the fruit, he would begin to die, and that death would be consummated in a complete death, both spiritually and physically. Adam did die spiritually, in the loss of primitive holiness, and though his body lived nearly a thousand years, yet it at last yielded to mortality. Now the first death is that which is entailed upon us by the fall of our first parents. Death nowhere means annihilation, but simply the separation of any living being or organ, from its true foundation of life. Hence spiritual death is the separation of the human spirit from God, who is the ceaseless fountain of holiness and love, and when the soul breaks company with the Spirit of God, and loses inward purity and holy love, it enters a state of soul death. And the death of the body consists, not in the destruction of a single particle of the bodily organism, but in the separation of the body from the animating soul which inhabits it. A piece of plank was once a living tree, but it has been separated from the vital sap which once flowed in it, and is dead, but not one atom of it is annihilated. So Satan and all his evil angels, were once in their primitive creation in fellowship with God, but they have broken union with the eternal fountain of love, and are utterly dead in sin, and filled with iniquity, yet not annihilated, nor have any of their original faculties or capabilities been destroyed, but are utterly perverted in a life of sin. Hence the iniquitous heresy of the annihilation of men's souls is a delusion of Satan, and comes from an ignorant confounding of the term death, with non-existence. Now this first death, which comes from Adam, both morally and physically, has been atoned for by the incarnation and death of the Son of God. So that no human being will ever be finally lost because of Adam's transgression. Jesus has purchased, by His sufferings and death and resurrection, an absolute indemnity from the fall of Adam, making ample provision for all of the consequences of Adam's transgression, both for the removal of all original sin. and the raising again from the dead every human being. Every infant born in the human race comes into being under the covenant of redeeming grace. We are expressly told that, "as in Adam all died, so in Christ shall all be made alive." From this we learn that the iniquity of Adam, as an open transgressor, is not imputed to any infant in the form of actual guilt, and that the principle of indwelling sin, which is in the infant, has its ample remedy in the shed blood of Jesus, and if the infant dies before reaching the age of accountability, its nature is thoroughly purified, on the basis of the covenant which the Son of God made with the Father, as the second Adam, and true head of the race. Thus we see that of all the millions of human beings, who may be finally lost, not one of them will be permitted to attribute his everlasting woe to our first parents. God will never allow any human being to attribute his ruin and perdition to another fellow-creature. He has dealt with the human race on such an enormous scale of mercy, and justice, and equity, and redeeming love, and impartiality, that every one will be compelled to attribute his ruin to himself. Thus the first death, both morally and physically, flows out from the first fall of the race of Adam, and the race have all been redeemed from that first fall, and that first death. Now let us remember that Jesus is the second Adam, and the second head of the race. If, when we come to years of accountability, we turn away from the Lord Jesus, "who is the second man from Heaven," and persistently turn away from Him, rejecting or postponing the salvation he offers us, and die in that attitude of rejection or neglect, we thereby fall a second time, and plunge into a second death. The apostle tells us that there is only one sacrifice for sins, and if we turn away from that one Savior, there can be found no other redeemer, but a fearful looking for of judgment, and of firey [sic] indignation from the Lord. This second fall, resulting from the rejection of Jesus, entails a second death in the utter separation of the soul from all fellowship with God, and all the touches of His grace, and also the banishment of the soul and body into the torments of hell, with the devil and his angels. We see that with regard to the first fall, and the first death, there is a limit. God's covenant of redemption rushes in to intervene, and stop the results that would naturally flow from the first fall, and the first death, in order that every creature may have the advantages of saving grace. The second fall and the second death have no limits to them, but their sad and awful consequences flow on forever. The same terms of duration which are used in Scripture concerning the destiny of the saved are also used concerning the destiny of the lost. There is no Greek word which exactly corresponds with our word "eternity," but the word used in the Greek Testament is that of "ages of the ages." And when it speaks of our having eternal life, it is that of living to the "ages of the ages," and these same terms are used expressive of the duration of the lost. It requires as much grace to keep us saved as it does to save us in the first place. In fact our continuance in salvation is but a prolonged and extended act of saving grace. So that when we are born of God, and eat of the tree of life, we are by faith to continue in the path of overcoming, lest we lose that life and drift away from the Lord Jesus, and fall into the second death. There are scores of scriptures which teach emphatically that after having once been saved, the soul may lose its grace and sink into utter darkness. In the 5th verse of the epistle of Jude, where our version says, "that after the Lord saved the Jewish people out of the land of Egypt, He afterward destroyed them that believed not,"' in the Greek it says, "that after he saved them from Egypt they were destroyed because they would not believe a second time," that is, they had faith to cross the Red Sea, but would not have faith to go into Canaan. And then the apostle Peter tells us (as translated in the common version) it were better for us not to have known the way of righteousness than after we have known it to turn from the holy commandment, but in the Greek it reads, it were better for us not to have known the way of justification, than after we have known it, "to turn from the commandment to be holy." This is exactly what thousands have done, commenced to live by faith, and been justified by faith, and then utterly rejected the commandment concerning holiness, and have forfeited all they gained, and in many instances they have utterly rejected Jesus and fallen into the second death. So this promise in the second overcometh is exceedingly vital. It requires an overcoming faith not only to be born again, but to keep from backsliding and falling into the second death.

Chapter VI
"THE HIDDEN MANNA"
Rev. 2:17

THE NEXT STEP in the series of qualifications for reigning with Christ is that of entering the second veil, and having access to the ark of the covenant, and eating of the hidden manna. Jesus says to the believer who reaches the third overcometh, "I will give him to eat of the hidden manna."

In this step we have the doctrine and experience of sanctification. Although holiness is not definitely mentioned in this verse, yet it is emphatically and fully expressed by emblem. Any truth set forth in Scripture by an inspired type is just as truly accurate as when set forth by a didactic statement. Thus we are taught in the Epistle to the Hebrews that the first veil represents regeneration, which is the beginning of the holy life, and that the second veil represents the perfecting of holiness and the full baptism of the Spirit as the shekinah flame between the wings of the cherubim. We see from the typology in this promise that the experience of sanctification is always placed, in Scripture, soon after the work of regeneration. The great mass of the nominal church have an impression that Christian holiness must come very late in life, that it is by the added growth of long years of Christian service, and many suppose it is hardly consciously received until about the time of death. But all such views are the result of mis-education, and of the natural unbelief of the human heart. Throughout all Scripture, both in precept and type, the blessed work of heart purity and the fullness of the Spirit are set forth as coming soon after conversion. Thus the crossing of the Red Sea is a type of the new birth, and the crossing of the Jordan is a type of sanctification, and we see from the history in Exodus it was God's design that the Israelites should not stay very long in the wilderness, but come up in a few months and possess the promised land. In like manner it is His expressed will that all young converts should come up soon after justification into the inheritance of the baptism of the Holy Spirit.

Also in the slaying of the passover lamb and the sprinkling of the blood upon the door posts we have a type of the penitent coming to Jesus to get under His shed blood. But it was just fifty days from that event to the Feast of Pentecost, or the baptism of the Holy Spirit, proving by clear Scripture type that the believer should receive the sanctifying gift of the Holy Spirit not later than fifty days from his justification.

The same truth is taught in manifold forms of expression and imagery in the Bible. Thus in these seven overcomeths we find the third step in the series to be a definite promise of sanctification. To understand the purport of this promise of eating the hidden manna more perfectly, let us refer back to the history of the manna in the writings of Moses. We there read that the manna fell on the open plain every night, and every morning the people gathered it up, and ground it and made it into cakes of bread. This manna was not hidden, but open to the gaze of all the people. When the Ark of the Covenant and the Tabernacle were constructed God told Moses to make a golden pot, and gather up some of this manna that lay on the ground and put it in the golden pot, and put the pot in the Ark of the Covenant, and put the Ark in the second veil, or the holy of holies. This manna thus preserved in the Ark was "the hidden manna." Now in order to eat any of that hidden manna a person must of necessity go through the first veil, which is the holy place, and then enter the second veil into the holy of holies. Thus we see that no one could eat of that manna except he entered into the second veil, which is nothing less or more than the state of entering heart purity and perfect love.

In this connection it will be very interesting to notice what were the contents of the Ark of the Covenant. We are taught both by Moses and Paul that the sacred Ark was a type of the Lord Jesus, the acacia wood being a type of His humanity, and the covering of pure gold a type of His divinity, that this Ark contained first the two tables of stone upon which God had written the ten commandments, and next the almond rod that Aaron held in his hand, and that budded and bore almonds, and next the golden pot containing the manna. Now all three of these things significantly set forth the living word of God. The tables of stone represent God's word in the form of law. The almond rod represents this word in the form of promise, and the hidden manna, sweet and nourishing to the taste, represents it in the form of fruition and experience.

Thus God's word comes to us first as an inflexible command, arresting us and putting us under conviction for our sins and the need of salvation. Next the message reaches us in the form of promise, with its buds and blossoms of hope and faith. Then the word comes to us as an inward conscious experience. That is the sweet manna. It is also worthy of notice, that each of these things in the Ark had a two-fold exhibition. The tables of stone were given twice. When Moses went down from the mountain, with the two tables containing the ten commandments, and saw the people in the act of idolatry, he dashed the tables to the ground, and they were broken. Afterwards God wrote the same words on two other stone tablets which Moses himself had to furnish. This sets forth the two covenants, the one in the flesh and the other in the spirit, referred to by Jeremiah and Paul. Then Aaron's rod was laid up all night before the Lord, and after it budded and blossomed, to distinguish him as the true priest from the false pretenders, the same rod was laid up a second time before the Lord. In this we see a type of the two works of grace. Also the hidden manna had two manifestations, one on the open ground from whence it was gathered every day, and then the hidden manna preserved in the Ark.

These things could not happen by chance, but all the details set forth unmistakably the two great works of saving grace, the one in saving from wrath, and the other purifying us for the heavenly life. The manna that fell on the ground would last only a day, typifying the transitoriness of the blessings and forms of nourishment in the lower state of grace, but the manna in the golden pot, kept sweet for a thousand years, indicating the permanent blessedness and richness of our spiritual lives while we dwell in the holy of holies and under the direct operation of the abiding Comforter. The manna is the very life of Christ, upon which all believers feed, and we must remember that the manna which lay on the ground every morning, and that which was preserved in the golden pot, were exactly alike, but each existed under different circumstances, and in a different relationship.

In like manner all believers live on the Lord Jesus, but there is a feeding on Christ in His outward life, and then there is an entering into His inner life, and by a thorough crucifixion with Him, and unlimited abandonment to His will, the soul enters into the inner region of Christ's spiritual life. Thus the apostle tells us that when we enter the holy of holies, we are to go through the veil which is the rent flesh of Jesus, by which we pass into His very heart life. And Jesus tells us that after we have found the first rest, we are to take His yoke upon us, and learn the secret of His inner being, that He is meek and lowly in heart, and then we shall find deep, permanent rest to our souls.

Thus the truth is spread out before us, under various forms of expression, that we are not merely to know Christ according to His outward life in the flesh, but to enter the secret recesses and fountains of His inner being, and know Him, in the language of the apostle, "according to the power of the endless life." This participation of the inner life of Jesus is the real hidden manna, which He offers to all those who are overcomers.

I may say in concluding this chapter that it is highly probable that the Ark of the Covenant was preserved at the time that the temple and Jerusalem were destroyed by Nebuchadnezzar, when the Jews were carried away into captivity. We read in the book of Maccabees in the Apocrypha, that God told Jeremiah to take some man with him, and take the Ark of the Covenant, with the curtains belonging to it, and carry it to the east of the Jordan, and hide it in a cave in Mount Nebo, where Moses died, in the place that God would show him, and cover the cave over with a stone, and that no one should discover it until the Lord should come to reign in His glory on the earth. And in the account which Jeremiah gives us of the capture of Jerusalem and the carrying away of the treasures of the temple into Babylon, He makes no mention of the Babylonians taking the Ark. Hence we have no grounds for doubting the accuracy of the account in the Apocrypha, and, if it be correct, then when Jesus comes and sets up His reign on this earth, that sacred

Ark, which was made at Mount Sinai, will be brought
forth from its hiding place and exhibited during the
millennial reign of Christ, as a proof and seal of God's
unbroken covenant with His saints in all ages.

Chapter VII
"THE WHITE STONE"
Rev. 2:17

THERE IS ANOTHER PROMISE included in the third overcometh, which is that of a pure heart, under the type of a pearl. Jesus says, "I will give to him that overcometh a white stone, and in the stone a new name written, which no man knoweth save he that receiveth it." This white stone can be interpreted by the words of our Savior, in which he says: "The Kingdom of Heaven is like unto a merchant-man seeking goodly pearls, who when he had found one pearl of great price, went and sold all that he had, and bought it." Here we see the pure heart, most beautifully illustrated under the typology of the pearl.

To get a clearer view of this emblem, let us note the following points:

1. The pearl is very valuable. They are obtained with great difficulty, and at a risk of life, and are sold for considerable sums. Jesus in His parable gives us to understand that one pearl could be of such magnitude and worth that a merchant would expend for it all of his goods

and all his wealth. This is pre-eminently true of the infinite worth of a pure heart. There are many treasures which human beings hold very dear, and in spite of their greed for material riches, yet when the test comes the great majority of mankind hold the treasures of good health, or of a sane mind, or of lofty genius, as paramount to mere material wealth. But God has taught us that a pure heart has in it a divine worth, which far exceeds all the riches of the material or intellectual world. Solomon gives in his Proverbs one of the finest climaxes in the Bible concerning the untold value of a pure heart, which he sets forth under the name of wisdom. He says that "it is better than silver," and then "superior to fine gold," and then "more precious than rubies," and then that "all the things the natural heart can desire are not to be compared unto it." The heart is the fountain of all moral and mental being. It is the inward spring, out of which flows all the diversified streams of life, and when the heart is thoroughly purified from every unlawful desire, and every unloving temper, so that out of its pure, pellucid depth there flows only the graces of the Spirit, which secures to its possessor advantages both in this life and the life to come infinitely above all price. He is the wise man who sells out everything in the world for this pearl.

2. The pearl is formed within a living creature. Pearls do not grow in the open air, or exposed to the beating elements. They are formed within an oyster, hidden away in the depths of the sea. Thus a pure heart is formed in the very centre of an immortal being. It is not an accident, that lies exposed to outward life. It is a living thing, and has its seat at the very centre of moral being.

3. The pearl is produced out of suffering, and by the crucifixion of a life. When the oyster opens its mouth to feed at the bottom of the sea, a small grain of sand is washed into it, which makes an incision in the soft part of the shell fish. In its effort, either to expel the

grain, or to heal the wound, it emanates a saliva, which is formed around the grain of sand, and makes the pearl. Thus our hearts are made pure, through the crucifixion of our natural life. Our inner being of self-will, and selfishness, must be pierced by the sharp word of God. There must be a breaking down of our thoughts, and plans, and ambitions, and selfish ease, and out of this interior crucifixion, which makes the heart to bleed, and the eye to weep, and the whole self-will to succumb to the authority of God, there is formed the blessedness and beauty of a clean heart.

4. The pearl has the character of remarkable beauty, among the precious gems of the earth. There is a delicacy, and softness of beauty about it, which far surpasses that of many gems, because it has been formed out of a living substance. In like manner, a heart that has been thoroughly washed in the blood of Jesus, and cleansed from all hardness, and bitterness, and impurity, and made soft and white and gentle by the power of the Holy Ghost, has in it a beauty which attracts the notice of the loving angels, and makes it as dear to God as the apple of His eye. No wonder that the infinite One himself has said, "that his eyes go to and fro throughout the whole earth, to show Himself strong, in the behalf of that person whose heart is pure and perfect toward Him." The eyes of glorified beings can sweep over a moral landscape, and read the different qualities of the moral universe, and see the different shades and degrees of holiness, as swiftly and accurately, as our eyes can discern the fascinating face of the magnificent landscape, or the exquisite colors and perfection of a flower garden.

The things that men prize highly in this world, are oftentimes an abomination in the sight of heavenly beings, but those who have perfectly humble and tender and spotless hearts, stand out to their gaze with extraordinary beauty and perfectness.

5. We are told in John's vision of the New Jerusalem that the gates of the City were each one of a solid pearl. All of the Bible emblems are selected with infallible propriety, and as a pearl is that thing in the world which beautifully represents a pure heart, so it is that thing which represents the gateway into the City of God, the Heavenly Jerusalem. In John's description of that City he says it was twelve thousand furlongs. This translated into our measurement would be about fifteen hundred miles. Think of a City of pure gold fifteen hundred miles square and fifteen hundred miles high, with three gates on each side, and each gate of one solid pearl fifteen hundred miles high and five hundred miles wide. Truly God is preparing something for His saints, the magnitude and glory of which will surprise the most extravagant dreams of earthly imagination. And yet vast and glorious as that vision is, we may each have in our own being, through the precious cleansing blood of Jesus, something which fully corresponds to it in a perfectly lowly and pure heart. A pure heart is the very gate to Heaven, and he who carries that gate of pearl within his own being will have no difficulty in obtaining an entrance to that City.

6. In this white stone Jesus promises to inscribe a new name which no one can know except the person receiving it. A name in Scripture is always indicative of a character, hence a new name is a new inward character, a divine and heavenly experience, which no one can know but the conscious soul in which it is wrought. Others may see the fruit of a pure heart and hear the testimony to that blessed work of grace, which has been accomplished in it, and they may be convinced of the reality of its existence, but after all there is an inward core of our being, into which no one can be admitted but our Creator and Redeemer and Sanctifier. Our loving Lord has, in beautiful wisdom, reserved to Himself the inner chamber of our immortal souls, the fountain of consciousness, the secret

source of character, and the home of moral intuitions. There is the secret fountain, where the Holy Spirit works the sweet miracles of saving grace. There are many marvelous things connected with our creation and existence, but none more so than the fact that God makes us each one to live a secret life with Himself. A life in which we are impenetrably walled in from all other creatures, and where He alone dwells, that is in the citadel of our nature. It is this "white stone" of inward purity that God offers to work into us if we by faith overcome.

Chapter VIII
"TILL I COME"
Rev. 2:25

THE PERSONAL COMING of Jesus back to this earth is everywhere set forth in the New Testament as the acme and crown and consummation of this present age. In all those passages where in the common version it speaks of the "end of the world," the Greek says "the end of the age." And if it had not been for the blunder of translating the Greek word "age" by the word "world," there would not have been so much darkness and misunderstanding on our Lord's return to reign on this earth. Just as the first coming of Christ in His incarnation was the end of the Jewish age, and all the types and shadows and forms of the Jewish ceremonial religion had their fulfillment and termination in the birth, life, death, and resurrection of Jesus, and after that the Jewish age with all its peculiar forms and ceremonies passed away, so the second coming of Christ back to this earth will be the end of the Gentile age, and the fulfillment and termination of all the present order in the Christian Church.

When our Savior instituted the sacrament which commemorates His death, we are told that every time we partake of that sacrament "we do show forth His death till he comes again." Hence the Lord's Supper is an index finger, pointing the believer throughout this age to the reappearing of his Lord. At the return of Christ all the Christian sacraments will come to an end, and also the present order of Christian ministry and the various forms of church government and manifold teachings of church theology. As all the streams flowing down the mountains find their terminus and rest in the bosom of the sea, so all the manifold streams of history in the present order of things will find their fulfillment and rest in the presence and personal reign of Jesus on this earth.

The Jews and Gentiles for the past two thousand years have had separate and distinct histories of their own, and we are told in the New Testament that Jerusalem, which embodied the nationality of the Jews, "should be trodden down of the Gentiles until the times of the Gentiles were filled." And St. Paul tells us in his epistle to the Romans that the Jews were cut off from the olive tree, and the Gentile believers, who were by nature the wild olive tree, were grafted into Christ, but that when the time of the Gentiles was ended the Jews should be again grafted upon the parent stock, which is Christ. Thus we see that at the appearing of our Lord these prophecies concerning the Jews and Gentiles will be fulfilled, and at His reign on earth the Jews will again be restored and accept of Him as their Messiah.

This idea may still further be elaborated in its application to Christian stewardship. Jesus, in addressing the church in connection with the fourth overcometh, says, "but that which ye have hold fast till I come," proving conclusively that there is a certain responsibility of faith and obedience in the believer, which does not terminate until the coming of the Lord.

The same truth is elaborated in the parables of Our Savior. We are told in the 19th chapter of Luke, that as Christ in His last journey approached Jerusalem, the people thought that the Kingdom of God should immediately appear, that is, they supposed Christ would then assume the kingship of His elect people, and set up His reign on the earth. Now we notice that Jesus did not contradict or deny the faith that He was to reign on this earth, but on the other hand, he confirmed that faith, by speaking a parable, concerning a certain nobleman who went into a far country to receive a kingdom, and before going away, he called his ten servants, and delivered unto them ten pounds, and said to them, "occupy till I come. Then He goes on to speak of the return of the nobleman, and of these ten servants rendering up their account, and to those of them who had been faithful, he said to one, "because thou hast been faithful, have thou authority over ten cities," and to another he said "have thou authority over five cities." This parable, and also the parable of the talents, proves that the stewardship of Christian ministers is to extend until the second coming of Jesus. Even though God's faithful servants may die before His appearing, yet their work follows them. They still live and labor in their writings, or through secondary agencies, and the amount of their reward for faithful service, or of their punishment for neglect of their gifts, will not be fixed, until the end of this age when Christ returns.

This gives us an insight into the vital relationship between the coming of Jesus and the winding up of the history and the various responsibilities and trusteeships of the present age. This truth has a still further application to Christian character and experience. Instead of regarding the coming of Jesus as a mere trifling matter which has but little connection with Christian faith and experience, we find in the New Testament that it is continually put as a fundamental object of faith and reward, and as having a powerful relationship with our present sanctification and fitness to see His face and participate in His coming kingdom. It seems that invincible narrowness of mind is one of the inevitable entailments of our fallen condition, and this narrowness of mind has had no more conspicuous exhibition than the divorcement of various truths in the Scripture which God has united, but which men have attempted to separate. A large class of people have in modern years become intensely interested in the personal coming of Jesus, but have studied that subject in a mere material and political aspect to the utter neglect of a deep experience in personal holiness. Many of them are mere materialists, denying the immortality of the soul, and either denying or utterly ignoring the necessity of a personal and full sanctification by the baptism of the Holy Spirit. On the other hand a large number of deeply spiritual persons who accept the full Bible teaching on personal and full salvation as a fitness for life, as well as for entrance to heaven, have entirely passed over the subject of our Savior's return to this earth, and of His personal reign over the nations for a thousand years. They have relegated the whole subject of Christ's coming to what is popularly called "Second Adventism," and in many instances spoken lightly or triflingly of the coming of Jesus, and with all their zeal and devotion for the spread of scriptural holiness, have stoutly maintained the Roman Catholic doctrine of post-millennialism, that is, that the church was to bring the millennium, and that Christ would not appear again until at the general judgment of both the saved and the lost. But when we look into the New Testament, we find both of these classes to be holding to mere partial truths. The Holy Spirit has blended these great truths into unity, and taught us in scores of places the direct connection between scriptural holiness and the pre-millennial appearing of our Lord.

Jesus teaches us in the 22d chapter of Luke the immediate connection between following Him in His humiliations and temptations, and the receiving of a place in His kingdom when He comes to reign on the earth. In the first chapter of Philippians, Paul gives us one of his apostolic prayers that the believers "may have the love of God abounding in them more and more, that they might be sincere and without offense until the day of Christ." Here is a statement of the direct relationship between the fullness of love and the preservation of the believer until the coming of Jesus. Again in the third chapter of Colossians the apostle tells us that we are to be dead to sin, and risen with Christ, and to seek those things which are heavenly, where Christ sitteth at the right hand of God, and that our affection is to be set on things divine, because our life is hid with Christ in God, and "that when Christ our life shall appear, then we shall appear with Him in glory." So here again the Holy Ghost has stated the supreme connection between a state of present holiness of heart and life and the personal appearing of our Lord.

Again in the First Epistle to the Thessalonians, Paul tells those believers that his hope and joy and crown of rejoicing, or as the Greek has it, his crown of glory, is in the perseverance of these saints until they meet in the presence of their Lord Jesus at His coming. In all these Scriptures there is no allusion to the death-bed, or the grave, as a terminal point of salvation, or stewardship, but everything focalizes "in the presence of Jesus." Again, in the same Epistle and third chapter, the apostle prays that the Lord would increase the love of the saints toward one another, to the end that God might establish their hearts without blame in holiness before God at the coming of our Lord Jesus Christ with His saints. Again in the fifth chapter he prays that the God of peace himself would sanctify us entirely, and preserve our whole spirit, and soul, and body, without blame, unto the coming of our Lord Jesus Christ. Thus the whole tenor of the New

Testament is: "Hold fast till I come;" "Occupy till I come;" "Render your stewardship when the Master returns;" "Be filled with love, and preserved without blame until Christ comes," and these two great facts of personal and full salvation and the second coming of Jesus are continually blended together.

We learn from the tenor of all these Scriptures, and similar passages in the Old Testament, that the presence of Christ himself constitutes the center and substance of His kingdom. For the first two centuries of the Christian era the Scripture teaching of the premillennial coming of Jesus was universally held among Christians. But when the Christian ministry began to lose the fullness of the Spirit, then their faith lost its strength and discernment, and they settled down on the plane of earthly politics and human philosophy, and as the church got more formidable and worldly, the doctrine began to be propagated that the Christian church was to conquer the nations of the world, and thus bring the golden age of prophecy without the personal presence of Jesus on the earth. And although the Protestant churches have thrown off the forms and many of the grosser teachings of Romanism, yet a great many unscriptural doctrines have sifted through from Romanism, and settled down as a sediment in the teachings of Protestantism to a much greater extent than Protestants themselves are aware of. One of these Romanist notions is that of the church conquering the world. When we look into the current views of modern worldly literature, we find a universal tendency to ignore God as a personal creator and governor in His works. The commonality of men are perhaps profoundly ignorant of the extent to which they ignore the existence and personality of the God who made them. And this is true of all classes of society, from the most polite to the most vulgar. The modern newspapers, magazines, and works of science, philosophy, literature, art, and history, are turned out by the thousand, and if every human being should suddenly die, and some inhabitant of a distant world should come here and look into these various literary productions, he would be astonished to find how utterly the God of the universe had been ignored in them all. Men speak of "nature" and "natural law" in a thousand ways without ever seeming to appreciate the thought of a living and personal Creator. And if God is mentioned, He is simply the masculine form of the neuter noun of nature. Now are we aware that a parallel sin is being committed, and has been for centuries committed by numberless multitudes in the visible church with regard to the Kingdom of God on this earth? Professed believers have imbibed the notion that the Kingdom of God will come about by various achievements of civilization and science, and modern progress, and ecclesiastical machinery, and that the kingdom consists merely in certain principles of reform and religious doctrine, while the personality and visible presence of Jesus as the center and embodiment of that kingdom seems seldom or never to enter the mind. Hence the church is looking for an impersonal kingdom of mere principles. But such a view of the coming of Christ's kingdom is utterly unscriptural, and nothing more or less than an anti-Christ, that is, the substituting of a church or a system of teachings for the personal presence of Jesus Himself. Just as the blazing sun comprises in itself the daily light and warmth of the earth, and the fruitful seasons, and the brightness of day, all flow out directly from the sun, so the Kingdom of God on this earth, the subjugation of the nations, the lifting of the curse from man and animals and material nature, the rectifying of earth's wrongs, and the filling of the world with the glory of God, all flow out from the person and presence of the Lord Jesus.

As men drifted away from God all their views became more and more impersonal, and they talked of principles and laws and forces. Hence we find Christian Scientists, and Spiritualists, and Free-thinkers ignoring a real personal Christ, but running off into a smoky haze of mystified thought in which they harp on "the Christ principle" and similar expressions of nonsense. But did we know that the church has committed this same blunder with regard to the kingdom of God on this earth, making it to consist of a universal spread of impersonal teachings and a conglomerate mass of churchism, instead of the presence of the personal King Himself, upon whose shoulder the government is laid, and out from whose person the empire flows? Hence men have unwittingly put the church in the place of the Lord Jesus, and there is a continual harping on "working for the church," "being sent out by the church," "being loyal to the church," "raising money for the church," "guarding the interests of the church," being "consecrated to the church," and "'making great sacrifices for the church," and all the while our adorable Jesus, Redeemer, Savior, Sanctifier, Healer, and coming King, is grieved to His heart to see how the nominal church has usurped His place in the hearts of men, and has assumed His throne and attempted to play the King in His stead. If in all of the fore- going expressions the word "Jesus" were used instead of the word "church," it would be according to Scripture. This putting the word "church" where the word "Christ" ought to be put is anti-Christ, for anti-Christ does not consist in a particular person, but in a vast multiplied system of the usurpation of the place of Jesus, and while anti-Christ may head up in some particular office as that of the Pope, yet it is spread out as a ubiquitous thing throughout fallen Christianity.

We read in Ezekiel that when God rebuked the kings of Judah for their idolatry, and prophesied their downfall, He says, "Remove the diadem and take off the crown and be abased, for I will overturn, overturn, overturn it, and it shall be no more until He comes whose right it is, and I will give it to Him." (Ezk. 21.) Here is a prophecy of the coming of the Son of God to govern this world, and the prophet does not say that *"it"* shall come, that is, an impersonal system of church government, but, emphatically till *"He"* shall come, the personal king.

It is in view of all these truths that the perfect believer is to set his heart on seeing Jesus, and loving His personal appearing. St. Paul gives us to understand that our love is not up to the New Testament standard until we have a perfect desire for the coming of Jesus, and that our whole heart loves His appearing.

Chapter IX
"POWER OVER THE NATIONS"
Rev. 2:26

AFTER TELLING US TO "hold fast till I come," Jesus proceeds to give a special promise to the saints, in connection with His coming and personal reign on earth, by saying, "He that overcometh, and keepeth my works unto the end, to him will I give power over the nations, and he shall rule them with a rod of iron. As the vessels of the potter shall they be broken to shivers, even as I received of my Father." Here is a most emphatic promise, of the rank and authority which those saints will have in Christ's millennial kingdom, who by their overcoming faith, shall be counted worthy of a place in His bridehood. This promise of the gift of power, has more than one fulfillment. Like other Scriptures, it must not be limited to only one application. It has a fulfillment in the spiritual life, during the present age, and will have its complete fulfillment in the coming age. In the present life, when a believer by faith overcomes all the works of Satan in his heart, he receives by the incoming of the Holy Spirit, a gift of power in the moral world over those who are around him. And although this enduement of power does not bring all the persons with whom he associates into subjection to Jesus, yet, notwithstanding, they feel the force of a holy heart and life, and as an individual unit he possesses his quota of power over the world. Many suppose that this is the only fulfillment which these promises have, but that is greatly to belittle the word of God. Those who do not believe in the pre-millennial coming of Jesus suppose from this Scripture that the nations of the world in their present state are to be subdued by the spiritual power in the hearts of what few believers there are who have a baptism of the Holy Ghost. But the Scriptures nowhere warrant this view. There is not a single text in the entire Bible which teaches that the nations are to be converted and saved in the present age or under the present order of things. The apostle tells us in the Acts that God is now "calling out a people for His name from among the Gentiles," and St. James tells us that the believers in the present age, "are a kind of first fruits," and we are told that the world, the ungodly portion of mankind, live in the hands of the wicked one, and that the wheat and the tares will grow together until the end of this age. The teaching of the word of God is that Christ is not only saving as many in the present age as He can, but that of these saved ones there is a special company who give themselves up entirely to God, and serve Him without any reservation, and who have in them the martyr spirit and the full baptism of the Holy Ghost, and these are technically called in Scripture "the elect," "the overcomers," "the bride of the Lamb, " "the church of the first born," or "the hundred and forty-four thousand," "those who are called and

chosen and faithful," and these are the ones who
are to be raised in the first resurrection, or caught
away at the appearing of Christ in the clouds of
Heaven, and glorified with Him, and sit with him
at the marriage supper of the Lamb, and then return with Him to this earth after the great tribulations, and sit with Him in His millennial kingdom,
and be appointed as prophets, and priests, and
princes, over all the earth to subdue the nations and
bring them into a state of holiness, and, with Christ,
rule over them a thousand years. There are scores
of Scripture passages which can not possibly have
any rational and satisfactory explanation except in
harmony with this statement. This promise of Jesus
we are now considering has no meaning except thus
interpreted. We know most assuredly that these
words where the overcomers are to have power over
the nations and rule them with a rod of iron, have
never yet been fulfilled. The ungodly have governed
this world from the fall of Adam, except for a few
brief years after the flood, when Noah and his family had charge of the depopulated earth. And we
also know that this Scripture can not be applied to
the Kingdom of God in the third heaven, where the
throne of the eternal Father is located, because there
are no sinful nations there to be conquered. Neither can it apply to the history of mankind beyond
the general judgment, for then all the saints and
sinners are forever separated. Hence we see that
the only period in the ages where this promise can
ever be fulfilled is during the millennial reign of
Christ on earth.

Some have supposed that at the second coming of Jesus
all the unsaved nations are to be destroyed and burnt up,
but if that were the case how could God's saints "rule
over the nations and break down their power like the

potter's vessel?" There is no Scripture that teaches that the nations of the earth are to be destroyed or killed at the appearing of Jesus. On the other hand, it is abundantly taught that they will remain here and pass through the terrific scourgings under the administration of the Ancient of Days.

In the parable of the ten virgins, those who have the oil, that is the Baptism of the Holy Spirit, will be taken away into the wedding banquet, and those who have lost their grace, or have not the oil, are left behind, but not destroyed.

Again Jesus presents three scenes in connection with His coming in the clouds. A night scene, two shall be in bed together, the one taken, the other left. A morning scene, two shall be grinding corn to prepare the morning meal, the one taken, the other left. A midday scene, two shall be in the field working together, the one taken, the other left. All these Scriptures prove that when the elect are taken up from the earth with Jesus in the clouds of heaven the people of the earth will be left, to live on and pass through the tribulations and propagate the human race, and when Jesus and His bride return from the wedding they will find the nations still living on the earth. Of course those who are taken away will be glorified like unto Christ, and Jesus says, they neither marry nor are given in marriage, but will be equal to the angels, and they are the ones who are to be His officers and sub-rulers in His millennial kingdom.

This is the exact teaching in the eighth Psalm that, when Christ reigns in all the earth, those persons who were perfectly humble, like little babes, shall be ordained with strength, and have power to still the enemy and the avenger. And further on in the Psalm that these saints were made for a short while lower than the angels, but will be glorified and crowned with glory, and honor, and have dominion over the works of God's hands, over all sheep, and oxen, and fowls of the air, and fish of the sea. That prophecy refers emphatically to Christ's millennial kingdom and the reign of His saints over the earth. The parallel of that Psalm is found in the second chapter of Hebrews. The apostle had stated in the previous chapter the doctrine of the ministry of angels during the present age over the heirs of salvation, but he says that the angels will not have charge over the habitable earth which is to come, that is in the coming age, but that these humble and holy men, who were made for a little while lower than the angels, and who have been sanctified and made one with Jesus, are to be crowned with glory and rulership in the coming age.

Compare Heb. 1:14 with second chapter, verses 5 and 11. In the forty-fifth Psalm we have a marvelous portrait of Jesus as a king, and of the elect saints as His queen, standing at His right hand, dressed in the gold of Ophir, and in the close of the Psalm we are told that the members of this queenhood are to be "sent forth as princes in all the earth." That Scripture has never yet been fulfilled, except in a very limited sense, of those apostles and evangelists who have gone through the earth saving souls, but they have never been princes over all the earth, even in that sense, but only over a few penitent and believing souls in a moral way.

We have a similar prophecy in Psalm 46, giving a description of the desolation which God will make in the earth during the great tribulations, and then He will make the wars to cease unto the end of the earth, and break the bow, and cut the spear in sunder, and burn the chariot with fire, and make the nations to be still, and to know that He is God, and that He will be exalted among the heathen in the earth. That Scripture has never yet been fulfilled, and the only time it can possibly be accomplished will be when Christ and His glorified saints take charge of the world. In Psalm 47 we have another inspired pic-

ture of the Lord Jesus as being king over the earth, and
the psalmist says: "He shall subdue the people under us,
and the nations under our feet." That Scripture has never
yet been fulfilled; on the other hand, the people have kept
the saints of God under, and the nations have put their
feet upon God's holy ones. But the day is coming, and
that speedily, when these words of the psalmist will be
literally and abundantly fulfilled.

   In the thirty-second chapter of Isaiah we are told that
"a king shall reign in righteousness, and princes shall rule
in judgment, and a man, that is a glorified man, shall be
as a hiding place from the wind, and a covert from the
tempest," which corresponds with the teaching of Paul
in the second of Hebrews that the glorified saints are to
be the custodians, and guardians, and protectors of the
people who will be born in the millennial age, just as angels are now our guardians and protectors. And to show
that this prophecy in Isaiah refers directly to Christ's
millennial kingdom it is in connection with the prophecy
in the previous chapter, and "that day when men will
cast away their idols of silver, and idols of gold, and when
the Lord shall lift His ensign in the earth, and put his fire
in Zion, and His furnace in Jerusalem." We read in the
seventh chapter of Daniel "that the saints of the most high
shall take the kingdom, and possess the kingdom forever, even forever and ever." And to prove that this refers
to Christ's coming reign, he says in the same chapter that
the kingdom shall be under the whole heaven, and shall
be given to the people of the saints of the most high, whose
kingdom is an everlasting kingdom, and all dominions
shall serve and obey Him. This prophecy has certainly
never yet been accomplished, and we notice that the reign
of the saints of the most high is put in this prophecy, as
also in that of Isaiah, right in connection with the reign
of Christ Himself, that is, the glorified saints are to share
the kingdom with Christ, and to be rulers under Him.

The word "horn" in Scripture always signifies "government," dominion, and Daniel says in the same chapter: "I beheld, and the horn of the beast made war with the saints, and prevailed against them." We know this Scripture has been fulfilled for many centuries, and especially when the beast of Romanism prevailed against the saints in the dark ages, and this prevailing of the beastly horn against the saints still goes on, and Daniel says will go on until the Ancient of Days come and judgment is given to the saints of the Most High, and the time comes that the saints possess the kingdom. That prophecy of Daniel corresponds exactly with this promise in the second of Revelation, that Christ will give power to His overcoming saints over all the nations of the earth to rule them with a rod of iron.

We read in Malachi that when the Lord shall come as a blazing sun of righteousness, with healing in His wings, then those who love and fear Him shall go forth as calves of the stall, and shall tread down the wicked like ashes under the soles of their feet. In order to get a more correct understanding as to who these are that shall go forth as calves of the stall to tread down the wicked, they are described in the previous chapter where it says: "They that feared the Lord spake often one to another, and the Lord hearkened and heard, and a book of remembrance was written before Him," "and they shall be mine, saith the Lord of Hosts, in that day when I make up my jewels." The word "jewels" in our common version is in the original "my special treasures," distinctly indicating the class of believers entirely devoted to God. These are the saints that shall be gathered out in the day of the Lord, and the prophet goes on to say that these saints shall return, that is, come back with Jesus from the wedding supper, and discern between the righteous and the wicked, that is, they will be judges, with the gift of discerning the spirits and superintending and controlling the nations that are

IX: "Power Over the Nations"

still living on the earth. Jesus says in Matthew, 24th chapter, "that those faithful servants who shall be found feeding the household of Christ with the meat of a pure gospel at the time of His second coming shall be blessed; and Christ declares He will make such servants rulers over all His goods. Jesus means exactly what He says, that such servants shall be His princes over the earth during His reign.

Also in the 22d chapter of Luke, Jesus affirms that those disciples who have continued with Him in His temptations, not those who began and fell out by the way, and not those who continue with Him in luxury and ease, with light work and large salaries, but those who persistently cling to Him through trouble, and sorrow, and loneliness, and temptation, and come off as overcomers, He says to such, I will appoint unto you a kingdom, as my Father has appointed unto me, that you may eat and drink at my table in my kingdom, and sit on thrones judging the twelve tribes of Israel.

What horrible work a great many church teachers make of this Scripture, in trying to twist it into a Swedenborgian mystical meaning. The infinite Christ does not trifle with His people, and means exactly what He says, and just as infallibly as God the Father hath appointed a kingdom to His Son, so as infallibly, Jesus will appoint His victorious followers, who serve Him with perfect loyalty, a kingdom, and give them thrones, and principalities, over the nations of the earth. Here is a definite prophecy that the twelve tribes of Israel will, during that kingdom, be restored, and put under the jurisdiction of glorified apostles.

The same truth is set forth in the 5th chapter of Revelation, where the "four living creatures," who represent glorified saints, sing a new song unto Him who was slain, and hath redeemed them by His blood, and hath made them kings and priests, and concludes by saying, "and they shall reign on the earth." This is an emphatic statement, that the kingdom referred to is not in some distant world, but on this very earth where they had been redeemed. Another proof text is found in Revelation twelve, where the man-child, which does not represent as some suppose the Lord Jesus, but which signifies the indefatigable martyrs slain by the red dragon of the Roman inquisition, and these martyrs, it is said, shall rule the nations with a rod of iron; that is, they will form a part of the bridehood of the Lamb, and come back with Him to govern the world. Another proof text is found in Revelation twenty, concerning those who are counted worthy of a place in the first resurrection, where it is said, "blessed and sanctified are they that have part in the first resurrection, for they shall be priests of God, and of Christ, and shall reign with Him a thousand years."

These Scriptures are all clear, specific, and unanimous, and there are scores of other passages that could be cited to prove the same truth. The significance of the expression, "to rule the nations with a rod of iron," will be considered in a future chapter, when we come to the setting up of the theocratic throne of our Savior in Jerusalem.

Chapter X
"THE MORNING STAR"
Rev. 2:28

ANOTHER STEP IN THE QUALIFICATIONS for reigning with Christ in His coming kingdom, is that of having "the morning star." All the metaphors of the Bible are used with infallible precision, and we can learn the mind of God by studying them. When Jesus is compared to a blazing sun, it always refers to His visible, personal appearance, the open manifestation of His Majesty, either in heaven to angels and glorified saints, or else to His incarnate history while on the earth, or else to His "parousia;" that is, His personal appearing in the clouds of heaven. But when Jesus is compared to a "star," it refers to the interior and spiritual manifestation of Himself by the Holy Spirit in the mind of a perfect believer. It will greatly aid us in understanding many prophecies of Scripture, and also in our experiences, to keep these metaphors clear in our thought.

Jesus as a "star" enters into our hearts, and unveils Himself to us privately and personally. Jesus as a "sun" comes to us outwardly and visibly, manifesting Himself to the world-at-large, the collective mass of His children. Hence when Jesus, as the divine Bridegroom, comes to collect the great body of His saints to Himself, He will come as a blazing Sun, eclipsing all other creatures in heaven and earth, and filling the spaces of the sky with His dazzling brightness. But before that glorious event, He reveals Himself to the eye of pure faith, as the individual Bridegroom of the heart, as a sweet, brilliant morning star, coming to us in the night of our present life, and by the Holy Spirit, unveiling Himself in a private, personal, and transcendent manner, as the one altogether lovely.

There is a logical connection in the promise between the gift of power and the gift of the morning star. The gift of power over the nations has a preliminary and spiritual fulfillment in the baptism of the Holy Ghost on the perfect believer, and it is by this baptism of the Spirit that Christ is revealed in the heart, in the glory of His divine and personal character. In the 14th chapter of John, where Christ promises to give the abiding Comforter, He adds to the promise, "In that day ye shall know that I am in the Father, and the Father in me," that is, that under the illumination of the indwelling Comforter there will be revealed to our inner consciousness the perfect divinity of our Lord Jesus, and of His unity with the Father. Hence in this promise, which we are now considering in this second chapter of Revelation, after promising to the overcoming saint power over the nations, He adds the other promise of giving to the overcomer the morning star.

In tracing out some further thoughts on this subject let us notice:

1. That the morning star is revealed in the night. Hence it refers to Christ being manifest during what has been appropriately called "the night of faith." It is in accord with this Scripture that the personal visible presence of

Christ in the world is always denominated "the day," while His absence from the earth is called night. When Jesus was on the earth He said: "Yet a little while is the light with you. While ye have the light walk in it, lest darkness come upon you." Again He said, "I am the light of the world." The apostle says, "The night is far spent, the day is at hand," meaning by "night" the absence of Jesus from the earth, and meaning by "the day is at hand" the near approach of our Lord's personal coming. Again He says, "Exhort one another daily, and so much the more as ye see the day approaching," meaning by the approaching day the return of Christ to fill this world with His glory and kingdom. The psalmist tells us that "the upright shall have dominion over the wicked in the morning," meaning by the word "morning" the beginning of Christ's reign on this earth. The words can have no other significance, for it cannot apply to the third heavens, as there are no wicked people there. It can not refer to hell, for there are no upright persons there, and it can not refer to the present order of things, for wicked men now rule this world, and there can be no period for the fulfillment of this prophecy, except in that bright morning of the millennial age, when Jesus and His saints shall possess the kingdom. Persons who speak in a lofty strain of the light of Christian civilization as being the noonday of Bible truth, while the world everywhere is mantled in spiritual darkness, and the muddy waters of worldliness are inundating the visible churches, and while sinners are multiplying ten times faster than the saints are, can have no real conception of what God means by the word "day." They speak after the manner of men, and mistake the twilight of civilization for the glorious day of spiritual light.

While a small number of holy saints are being internally illuminated by the morning star revealed in their hearts, the world at large, even the most cultured of those who have not the baptism of the Spirit, are walking at best in the pale moonlight reflected from true believers, but still they are plodding along in the night, dreaming it is meridian day. When God uses the word day, He measures it by His own thought of what day is, and not by the groping conceptions of carnal minds. Hence the Word of God speaks over and over again of "the day of Christ," and "the day of God," and of "that day," as if all the light that men now have was midnight in comparison.

2. The morning star will bear some comparison with the other stars in the sky, though it outshines them all. But when the sun rises, there is no comparison between it and the other luminaries in the heavens, for all other celestial and terrestrial lights are pale behind its splendor. In like manner, during the night of faith, Jesus is revealed to the pure in heart, in His spotless humanity, as the brightest and most attractive of all beings in the universe. Even if we consider His blessed humanity apart from the divinity of the Eternal Word, still there is a beauty and lustre in that human nature surpassing all the starry hosts of angels and saints, for the Holy Spirit not only reveals His absolute divinity, but also the incomparable beauty and loveliness of His humanity. Every saint of God is a real form of heavenly beauty, which far surpasses the most beautiful objects in material creation, and when we turn our thoughts upon that bright land of angelic and glorified spirits, could we see them in all their multiplied variety and their individual graces and charms, it would doubtless dazzle our under-standing; but were we able to survey all those myriads of legions and comprehend their graces and beauties in one collective mass of glory, the whole scene of exquisite loveliness, multiplied millions of times, would not equal the ineffable beauty and glory of the crucified and glorified humanity of Jesus. It has pleased the Father that in that humanity all the fullness of God should abide.

This inward revelation of Jesus as the morning star is referred to by St. Peter in his second epistle, where he refers particularly to the second coming of Christ as typified by the transfiguration, and says that when he was with Christ in the Holy Mount he there "saw the power and coming of our Lord Jesus Christ," and then goes on to say that "we are to take heed to that word of prophecy, which is like a lamp shining in a dark place, until the day shall dawn and the Day Star arises in our hearts." The "day dawn" is the work of regeneration, and the "Day Star arising in our hearts" is the work of the sanctifying Spirit cleansing away our natural darkness and revealing Jesus as a perfect Savior within us.

St. Paul, in the first chapter of Galatians, mentions three epochs in his life. First, his natural birth; second, his conversion; and third, the sanctifying baptism of the Spirit revealing Christ in his heart. He says: "It pleased God, who separated me from my mother's womb, and called me by His grace, to reveal His Son in me." In this sentence the verbs "separate," and "call," and "reveal" are all in the aorist tense, which always indicates in the Greek language instantaneous events. Thus the revelation of Christ in the heart of St. Paul is what Peter means by the day star arising in our hearts, and the same thing that Jesus means by saying, "I will give him the morning star." Hence Christ, as the Day Star, is a peaceful, sweetly pining vision of faith, for the fullness of His glory. It is a love for Himself personally, a heart embracement of His adorable person, a being mentally charmed with the exquisite grace of His character, a gentle sinking down of our will along all lines into His will, a divine intuition of His lamblike and dove- like nature, a quick and loving surrender day by day of all our judgments, and prejudices, and labors, and sufferings, and circumstances to the inward sway of His gentle nature, and a glad placing of our souls and bodies, with every affection, hope, and want, under the gentle pressure of His loving foot, and a secret grief at seeing Him so little appreciated, and so unloved by His own creatures. It is a sweet longing to see Him reigning as absolute monarch over everybody and everything. It is an earnest love for His appearing, and a desire to nestle close up to Him when He comes in glory. It is an inexpressible Holy Ghost passion for the man Christ Jesus, the incarnate one of God.

When Jesus is spoken of as coming in the clouds of heaven, He is then compared to a blazing Sun. Malachi prophecies of that event by saying: "Unto you that fear my name shall the Sun of Righteousness arise, with healing in his wings, and ye shall tread down the wicked as ashes under your feet." And John declares that "Jesus will come in the clouds of heaven, and every eye shall see Him, and all kindreds shall wail because of Him." Now we must remember that no one will be prepared to meet Jesus as a blazing Sun coming in the clouds of heaven unless he has previously been purified by His precious blood and had Christ revealed within him as the Morning Star. Thus as the morning star, on the brow of the approaching day, indicates the rising of the sun, so the revelation of Jesus, as a perfect personal Savior within the heart, gives us prophetic intimations of His coming as a glorious king, and prepares us for that transcendent event. Through all the Christian generations, when believers have reached the degree of grace which admits them into the number of the bridehood of the Lamb, they have had this gift of the Morning Star, this fascination for the face of Jesus, which is the Holy Ghost photograph of the divine Bridegroom, which He sends on ahead of His appearing, and hangs it up in the hearts of those who are to sit with Him at the marriage supper, and share His royal prerogatives in His coming empire.

In reading the biography of holy persons we are struck with the fact that when they have reached a certain degree in grace they have had this inward spiritual vision of Jesus and wonderful premonitions of His second coming. As a sample of what thousands of saints have felt in days past, I will quote a beautiful instance from the writings of the saintly Faber: "Before the dawn of day a huge rolling mass of unwieldly cloud came up from the western horizon. With incredible swiftness, and the loud roaring of sudden wind, it covered like a pall the brilliant moonlit heavens and deluged the earth with slanting columns of whirling rain. It passed on. A star came out, and then another, and at last the moon, and then the storm drove onward to the east, towards the sea; and all at once a lunar rainbow spanned the black arch of heaven, and it seemed as if Jesus should have come beneath that bow and through that purple cloud that was barring the gates of the sunrise. And what is all this but a figure of our lives, of which we might make so much?"

There is a class of religionists who make a specialty of the second advent, but whose teachings are largely materialistic, denying the immortality of the soul and the divine personality and sanctifying work of the Holy Spirit and other Scriptural truths. If Christ should appear, such persons would be utterly unprepared to meet Him. Unless we have within us the Morning Star we are in no condition to meet the blazing Sun. The Scriptures nowhere teach that the moment of Christ's appearing will be a moment for the purifying of our nature, or for the filling of us with the Spirit, but it will be a moment for catching away those who are already made pure in heart and filled with the oil, and who have in them Christ abiding as the Morning Star.

This is definitely referred to in the language of the elect woman, in the Song of Solomon, where she says, "My beloved is mine and I am His. He feedeth among the lilies until the day break and the shadows flee away. Turn, my beloved, and be thou like a roe or a young hart upon the Mountains of Bether," or, as it should be rendered, "Upon the Mountains of Separation." In this passage there is indicated a blessed, deep union between Christ and His elect, and the invisible Jesus is represented as coming down in the Spirit, in the humble valleys of earth, and feeding Himself upon the love of His own saints, who are compared to lilies, and this communion will go on until the daybreak of His second coming and the shadows of this present age have flown away before that rising Sun. And the loving believer is pleading for the Bridegroom to hasten His coming over the mountains that separate between this wicked age and the golden age of His millennial reign.

There are doubtless many prophetic events and acts in the life of our Savior when on this earth, which we have never yet discovered or appreciated. The smallest things in the incarnation and life of Jesus have a transcendent [sic] and far-reaching meaning which surpasses all our thought. Among them we may notice that for several months the Eternal Son of God enshrouded Himself with His earthly mother before coming forth in visible manifestation to reveal the Father to the human race, and to make an atonement for the sins of men. During those mysterious months of the incarnate Word of God no one can tell the thoughts and feelings of the humble Mary, how her thoughts turned almost every moment to her incarnate Lord, and how she lovingly and wistfully pined for the hour to come when she might look upon that most lovely face in all the creation of God, that face which should show forth more of the glory of the three persons of the Godhead than all the faces of angels or men combined, and how she yearned to kiss those lips that should speak the doom of all mankind. Even as an unborn Infant, He had power to sanctify John the Baptist, and to fill him with the Holy Ghost before his birth, and to fill his mother, Elizabeth, with the Holy Spirit. (Luke, 1st chapter, 39, 45). Is not all this a divine parable of what is now taking place? Christ is to be now formed within our hearts, the hope of glory, to live within us in His personal, forgiving, cleansing, and comforting presence, just as really as His humanity lived in His earthly mother, and, like Mary, the more we comprehend this blessed indwelling of Christ in our hearts, the more we are filled with premonitory leapings of soul in anticipation of the hour, when we, too, shall see that face that she longed to see. As the hour of His coming draws near, His true, anointed ones in all the earth will feel more intensely growing within them this prophetic feeling of seeing Him in glory.

Chapter XI
"WHITE RAIMENT"
Rev. 3:5

As we come to consider the next step which is set forth in the promise of the fifth overcometh, we find the manifestation of the Christ-life taking on a still further development in that of a perfect testimony. "He that overcometh the same shall be clothed in white raiment, and I will not blot out his name out of the book of life, but I will confess his name before my Father, and before His angels." These words cover the entire range of Christian testimony, and also the counterpart of our testimony on earth, which is Christ's testimony for us in heaven. This promise of being clothed in white raiment expresses the full confession both by lip and outward life of the work of grace in the heart. The white stone is pre-eminently expressive of a pure heart, the hidden work of God within the soul, but the white raiment is expressive of outward manifestations of that inward whiteness in the words, manners, and all the features of outward life. We may gather from this promise the following points:

1. God has so constructed all living things that they will tell on themselves. What is in the heart of any creature will inevitably come to the surface and make itself known. Life in itself is always hidden, and can never be discerned by the microscope. But life of every kind has in it a quality of revelation so that everything will sooner or later bear outward testimony of its inward nature. And this outward expression of the inward life takes on the form of a garment. The inward life of a fish will manifest itself in outward fins and scales, and makes up the garniture of its peculiar organic life. The hidden life in the blood of a bird will confess itself in the plumage of the bird, and this outward plumage in color and texture is an infallible confession of the species of life within. The secret life of a tree, which lies in its sap, could not be distinguished under a microscope as to its genus or species, but let that sap come forth in bud, and bloom, and foliage, and at once the secret of its inner nature is made known. Man might take a swine and shave him clean, and cover him with white wool, but just as long as the swine blood lives in its heart it will grow bristles.

This great fact of creation is manifested everywhere, that "the blood will tell" —the inward life will clothe itself outwardly in an exact and corresponding raiment. This is as infallibly true of the soul as of any other form of life. It is eternally impossible for the secret life of the immortal soul to remain long concealed, and the outflow of that life, in words, and tempers, and tones, and gestures, and business transactions, will sooner or later be an exact manifestation of the secret fountains of the hidden life. It is God Himself who has established these unchanging laws, and they are but the outworking of His absolute equity and justice and love. Hence He says that the overcoming believer, who has the white stone of a pure heart and the Morning Star of an indwelling Christ, will have the outward clothing of a humble, pure, gentle, discreet, bold, and heavenly life, which is the spotless garniture growing out from interior whiteness, with as absolute precision as a lamb's heart with its lamb's blood will clothe itself with lamb's wool. This white raiment will take on more intense forms of brightness, and sweetness, and outward glow in life, according to the intensity of the pure love in the heart. We are told that "God covers Himself with light as with a garment." From which we learn that the manifestation of the Godhead to glorified spirits is that of the infinite ocean of inexpressible fire, a flame of light so excessively bright that Paul says no man can approach unto it—that is, no man in this mortal state could endure the sight. It would seem that God wants to raise us into fellowship with Himself, and so fill us that we also shall be clothed in a white fire.

We read of the living creatures in Ezekiel that they were like lightning, and that fire flashed out from them. We read of angels appearing to prophets as young men, clothed in white raiment of dazzling brightness. We also read of Jesus on the Mount of Transfiguration, letting the inward glory shine out through His raiment, making it of dazzling whiteness, and also of Christ being revealed to His prophets as clothed in white raiment, with His eyes like lightning, His face like the sun, and His feet like glowing brass in a furnace. The glorified saints are to be made like unto their Lord, so that in the future age they will be as radiant living flames.

If all this be true, then even in this life there must be a beginning of all these things, and so it comes to pass that the perfect believer can be filled with the love of God, like a glowing furnace, and have his inner spirit clothed with the Holy Ghost like a shining mantle. Hence there are times when under this spiritual investure of white fire the face will shine, the eye will flash, the voice have a mellow, penetrating sweetness, and the manners melt into such lowliness and grace as to almost make the white robe of the inward soul visible to the eye.

2. "I will not blot out his name out of the book of life." This indicates clearly that it is possible, at least up to a certain point in Christian progress, for a believer to apostatize and have his name stricken from the book of life. Why should God use words that have no meaning, and if it were impossible for real believers to have their names blotted out, why should God say so? No human theology in this world expresses the whole of any Bible truth. The doctrines of Calvinism and Arminianism equally fail to express the whole truth. While the Scriptures teach most positively what is commonly called the final perseverance of the saints, it at the same time teaches just as positively that real, genuine believers whose names were in the book of life have apostatized and gone into outer darkness. It is not for us to formulate God's infinite Bible into an inflexible creed. In the thirty-third chapter of Ezekiel, God emphatically declares that the righteous man who is really righteous may turn away from his righteousness and commit iniquity, and die in that state, and that then all his righteousness shall not be mentioned. And that a wicked man may turn away from his wickedness and become righteous, and if he lives in that state his sins shall never be mentioned unto him. And the Apostle Peter tells us it were better for a man not to have known the way of righteousness than, after he has known it, to turn from the holy commandment, or as it should be rendered, to turn from the commandment to be holy.

So there is a point in grace from which man may apostatize, and then we are taught in the verse now under consideration that there is a point in grace which fixes the destiny of the soul eternally for glory. And Christ affirms that when the believer reaches that point in spiritual progress, indicated in this fifth overcometh, that his name will never be blotted out from the book of life.

3. Jesus says: "I will confess his name before my Father and before His angels." So there are two testimonies transpiring—one on earth, a testimony for Jesus, and one in heaven, a testimony for the believer. As the believer by the outward expression in his words and manners, and prayers and definite confessions of saving grace makes known to mankind the indwelling of Christ in his heart, so Jesus, at the right hand of God the Father, is making known in the heavenly world, the fidelity and labor and true character of the believer on earth. This shows us the intimate relationship between the kingdom of God in grace and the King in glory. The perfect believer has Christ in him here in Spirit, and Christ carries that believer in His heart and in His mind at the right hand of the Father. The sympathies and inter-blendings of these two worlds are more blessed and perfect than many persons apprehend. The veil is very thin that separates between the Spirit-led child of God here and the radiant land of angels in heaven.

Spiritualism is Satan's counterfeit of these blessed and intimate relationships; and because of Satan's counterfeit, many timid and partially, or very weakly, illumined Christians, dare not grasp with their faith all the fullness of Bible statements on this subject. But Paul positively affirms in Hebrews, that the soul which has found its Pentecost in the Holy Spirit, has already come, even before the death of the body, into fellowship with the heavenly Jerusalem, and with an innumerable company of angels, and with the church of the first born, and with the judge of all men, and with the spirits of just men made perfect. If believers could see these things in true light, and apprehend Christ confessing them before the Father, how they would throw aside all their timidity, and backwardness, and half-cowardice, in confessing the cleansing blood, and come out in a life of great liberty and fullness in the Holy Ghost.

This verse has a parallel in the third chapter of Malachi, where we are told that, then those who feared the Lord spake often one to another; that is, confessed Christ fully and in sincerity, that the Lord hearkened, and heard their confessions, and a book of remembrance was written before Him, and the inference is plain, that in this book of remembrance, the confessions and obedience of His faithful children were recorded therein. The Bible tells of two books kept in heaven—one is the "book of life," and the other "the book of remembrance." The book of life simply contains the registry of the names of those who are saved, without reference to their degree and fervor of service; but the book of remembrance is a registry of all good works, and all the saints will be rewarded according to the records in this book of remembrance. We must never confound simple salvation itself with rewards, for we are told that many will be saved so as by fire, and their manifold works being erroneous, or only temporal, will be consumed by the fire, but that others who are saved will have great rewards. We understand that this confession of the names of the saints, which Jesus makes before the Father and His angels, involves something more than simple salvation from eternal death, it embraces a confession of their trials, the testings of their faith, their peculiar sufferings, their exhibitions of perfect loyalty, and their manifold labors, so that when Jesus comes to reward His holy ones, those rewards will be measured out with absolute equity, and infinitesimal propriety, which will be apparent to all the angels and the heavenly hosts. The rewards of those persons comprising the bridehood of Christ will be given at the marriage supper of the Lamb, which we shall consider in the succeeding chapter.

Chapter XII
"A PILLAR IN THE TEMPLE OF GOD"
Rev. 3:12

TO THE BELIEVER who advances as far in his spiritual progress as the sixth overcometh, Jesus promises, "I will make him a pillar in the temple of my God, and he shall go no more out, and I will write upon him the name of my God, and the name of the City of my God, which is New Jerusalem, which cometh down out of heaven from my God, and I will write upon him My new name." Just before making this promise, in His address to the same church, He says, "Behold, I come quickly. Hold fast that which thou hast, that no man take thy crown." This announcement that He will come quickly is made to the church at Philadelphia, and as there was only one more church to be addressed, that of Laodicea, which represents the lukewarm condition of the present Protestant churches of the world, we understand that the coming of the Lord is very near. It would also seem, from the connection between the warning that no man take our crown and the promise of making us pillars in the temple of God, that there was an intimate relation. As we see, each of these promises to the overcoming Christian lies in an ascending climax, and the soul that has passed through the steps of experience and life indicated by the previous overcomeths is now prepared to enter into a deeper union with God, and be incorporated into the interior structure of His kingdom more firmly and abidingly than ever. To be a "pillar in the temple of God" indicates that the soul has penetrated from the outer courts of religious life into the very center of that glorious spiritual structure which the Holy Ghost has been fashioning through the centuries. It indicates a state of spiritual life which is thoroughly rooted in God, and everlastingly fixed in a calm, sweet union with the divine attributes and the divine character. A pillar in a temple is one of its interior and essential portions upon which the structure largely rests, which gives character, support and beauty to the building.

The Scriptures reveal to us in many places that God is forming a veritable and living temple composed of regenerated and sanctified souls throughout the centuries, which are denominated real "living stones," and that the Holy Ghost is building these purified natures up into a real living city or temple, and that every soul entering that structure has its appropriate place with as much accuracy and reality as the stones of a real palace which have been previously carved and fashioned in the quarry for their several places in the building. Paul expressly says that true believers are God's building, they are His temple. Peter says that we are to taste that the Lord is gracious, and that as living stones we are built up a spiritual house, a holy priesthood, which indicates that the house is a real living temple.

At the bottom of the sea myriads of little coral insects

begin to build themselves up unitedly in the coral reef. For long centuries the structure goes on increasing, but all hidden beneath the dark, green waters of the sea. At last the coral reef rises above the surface of the sea, and becomes visible to the eye, and soon it is covered with gorgeous foliage and tropical products. In like manner, through all the centuries past, and hidden away from physical eyesight, and the reason of carnal men, God has been working upon a marvelous structure, building for Himself a gorgeous temple, in which every stone is an immortal spirit, regenerated and purified, and filled with His own Spirit. This structure has not yet become visible, except perchance to the penetrating vision of angels and glorified spirits. But when Jesus appears and establishes His reign on the earth, this magnificent structure of myriads of immortal blood-washed souls will emerge from the dark waters of time, and become a visible, clearly cognizable structure in the eyes of angels and men. This is the city that Abraham saw in a vision, and that glittered down the long vista of faith to prophets and apostles.

The building of the temple by King Solomon, in which every stone was carefully finished in the quarry, and, when brought together, could be deftly joined together without the sound of a hammer, is an inspired type of the spiritual temple that is now being constructed by the Holy Spirit as a habitation for God. Now to be admitted as a pillar in that temple is a mark of great favor and honor from God. It is evident that all believers who enter into that glorious structure will not rank as pillars, for it would be out of keeping with all proper interpretation to suppose that every piece in the temple would be a pillar. And we notice that this promise was not given in the earliest stages of the overcoming life, but reserved for the last stage previous to sitting with Christ in His throne. There are thousands of degrees of grace among God's children. Having the heart purged from indwelling sin is the lowest stage of Christian perfection, and, after it, there is to come a great work of illumination in the understanding, and the revelation of spiritual things, and the manifesting of the three persons in the Godhead to the eye of the mind. And then there come, in the upper ranges of a life in the Holy Spirit, deep and interior experiences of divine union, where the faculties of the human spirit are brought into marvelous and unspeakable unity with God, where the understanding becomes enlarged and united to God's revealed word, where the affections are inexpressibly expanded and united to the sympathies and feelings of the Lord Jesus, and where the will, in all its choices and desires, is brought into a supernatural fixedness with the will of God, and with the movements of divine providence. These forms of the spiritual life are what we may understand by being so taken up into God as to be made a pillar in His coming kingdom.

In our further observations of this remarkable promise we notice:

1. That there is a state of Christian life set forth in the Bible, which fixes the believer's destiny forever. When it pleases God to take one of His servants and make him a pillar in the temple, Christ then affirms, "He shall go no more out." We are to take these words to mean just what they say. We have seen, in previous steps, that there are points in grace, from which the soul may retrograde, and be lost forever; but the Scriptures just as clearly teach, that there is a point in divine life where the believer's glorious destiny is forever settled. The same law applies to sinners as to saints. We are expressly taught by our Savior, that there were sinners to whom He spoke, who had gone so far in a life of disobedience that they had fixed their eternal destiny for hell. They saw Him casting out devils, and, right against all the light of reason, common sense, and conscience, they charged Him with being possessed with Beelzebub. Jesus told them that that was the

blasphemy against the Holy Ghost, that is, calling the work of the Holy Ghost the work of the devil, and doing it right against light. He then told them that that sin should never be forgiven either in this age or in the coming age, but that they should die in their sins, and where Christ was they could never come. This is an infallible declaration, that men may now put themselves where they never can or never will repent, and while walking upon the surface of this world, they are in reality a living portion of everlasting hell.

It is probable that the great majority of men now living on earth have passed this awful point of destiny, and that their eternal doom is just as really fixed as it will be at the judgment. Now what is true with regard to sinners is equally true reversely with regard to saints, that there is a point in Christian progress which absolutely fixes the believers destiny for glory, and honor, and immortality in heaven.

2. Jesus says that "I will write upon this pillar the name of my God." In the temples built for ancient kings in Egypt and Babylon there were large beautiful pillars upon which the reigning monarch would carve his name and the names of the various cities he built, and the battles which he fought, and his pedigree or dynasty. There have been preserved in the British Museum in London some of these magnificent pillars taken from the ruins of Eastern countries. I saw them when I was in London, and saw the carving upon them of the names and historical incidents of the ancient kingdoms. This is the very imagery referred to here in this text. When Christ says, "I will write upon Him the name of my God," it means that He will reveal to this perfect and established believer the most gracious and profound manifestation of the Fatherhood of God.

It is the Father who awakens us and leads us to His son Jesus, and then Jesus saves us, and leads us to the sanctifying baptism and indwelling personality of the Holy Spirit, and then the Holy Spirit leads us back to the Father, and gives us such a revelation of the person of the Father as the eternal fountain of all Godhead, as eternal and unchanging love, He gives us a view of His divine paternity in a far brighter and sweeter light than we ever knew in the earlier stages of initial grace. The highest stages in the Christ-life repeat over again what we learned in the early beginning, but in a much deeper and more luminous manner. What we need is to have the Fatherhood of God so engraved upon the vital centre of our being that we will continually have an abiding sense of Him as the person of the Father.

3. "I will write upon him the name of the City of my God, which is New Jerusalem." This is a remarkable promise, and refers to that special revelation which the Holy Spirit makes to the perfect believer of his being made a member of the bridehood of Jesus. To have the name of the New Jerusalem engraved in the life of the soul is to receive an inward experimental certificate from the Holy Ghost of being the "spouse" of the Lord Jesus. Young, or unestablished, Christians never receive this experience, and when they hear perfected believers speaking of that spiritual wedlock of their souls with Jesus, or talking in the style of the language of the Song of Solomon, they do not understand the real purport of such language. I have met many thousands of Christians, in all stages of experience, and I never remember of hearing any one speak in a serious and experimental manner of the subject of divine espousal, except those who had consciously and fully entered the baptism of the Holy Spirit. This is why the Song of Solomon is so little understood and so blunderingly interpreted by many. That Song expresses the high watermark of the spiritual life. And it has language and metaphors so flooded with supernatural experiences of personal affection for Jesus, and

yearnings after Him, which are all dry or gross hiero-
glyphics to believers who have not yet entered the sanctified bridehood of the Lamb.

Our Savior gives us to understand in the ninth chapter
of Matthew that there are some disciples who have not
yet come into the bridehood, and there are others who
have. The disciples of John said to Him: "Why do we fast
often, but Thy disciples fast not?" Jesus said unto them:
"How can the children of the bridechamber mourn as
long as the bridegroom is with them?" Now the disciples
of John were really the servants of God, but were serving
Him in a legal way, but those disciples who had left John,
and followed Jesus, had been lifted into the plane of a
love service, and Jesus calls them "the children of the
bridechamber," and says that His presence with them
was that of the bridegroom. This truth has a continual
and far-reaching application through all the Christian
centuries. There have ever been those who serve God really and truly, without entering that state of perfect heart-
union with Jesus which the Bible frankly expresses under
the type of marriage.

So when Jesus promises to write the name of the City
of God upon our hearts we are to understand that that
City is the same one referred to in Revelation 21, where
John expressly declares that the New Jerusalem made up
of the typical number of the hundred and forty-four thousand is the bride, the Lamb's wife. So the City is identical
with the bride, and hence the name of the City is identical with the name of the bride, and as we have seen a
name in Scripture represents character, and to have the
name of the bride, or City, written upon our hearts, is the
same thing as having the real, spotless, tender, loving
character of the bride of the Lamb engraved upon the
inner tablet of our consciousness. It is our privilege to
know, even in this life, these supernatural experiences of
grace, and to have, before we see His blessed face, the

perfect inward assurance that we are forever and forever the spouse of the Lamb.

4. "I will write upon him my new name." This new name is explained by the prophet Hosea, in which he describes the glory of God that shall fill the earth in the last days, and says: "It shall be at that time, saith the Lord, thou shalt no more call me *baali,*" which signifies my master, "but thou shalt call me *Ishi,*" which signifies my husband. This is the new name that Jesus will write into those who are filled with holy love. This writing consists of a pungent and sweet revelation to the soul of Christ's personal and individual love. In the lower degrees of grace we look upon the love of Jesus as of a general and universal character. But as we advance into closer union with Him, His love takes on clear forms of a special and personal character, and when we are perfectly crucified, and can say with St. Paul: "The life I live is not my own, but the life of Christ in me," then with Paul we can also say: "The Son of God *loved me* and gave Himself for *me,*" and this revelation of the personal affection Jesus bears for each of us makes Him more inexpressibly dear to us than all the outspread glories of Him in the general creation.

The word Lamb, as used in Revelation, is preeminently the name of Jesus as the heavenly bridegroom, and this word Lamb in every instance in Revelation is in the Greek *"arnion,"* which means a little, tender lamb. And so the last and highest revelation we have of Jesus is that of inexpressible gentleness and love. This is the name and the character which He will engrave in the consciousness of those who are perfectly established in union with Himself.

Chapter XIII
"I will Sup with Him"
Rev. 3:20

JUST BEFORE MAKING the promise in connection with the seventh overcometh, Jesus gives two preliminary promises which set forth His fellowship with us in the present state and our fellowship with Him at His heavenly banquet. Jesus is now visiting the churches on earth in this wide- spread revival of Christian holiness, and by this revival He is knocking at the door of all the churches and saying, that "if any man will open the door to Him, He will come in and sup with him." This sets forth that fellowship which Christ has with His disciples in their present state in the flesh that He comes down in the person of the Holy Spirit, and identifies Himself in all the affairs of life with the conditions and experiences of His followers.

If in walking through a field we pierce our foot with a thorn, instantly the nervous system, which is a perfect telegraphic arrangement, will notify the brain of the wound in the foot. If the brain were not thus notified, there would be no consciousness of pain in the foot. It seems that the suffering is in that part of the body pierced by the thorn, but in reality the suffering is in the brain, which is the center of the entire nervous system, and the center of all sensation. Instantly on receiving the dispatch from the afflicted member of the body, the brain comes down as it were into the foot, and enters into perfect sympathy with that member. The Holy Spirit has told us that Christ is the Head, and that His disciples, who are united to Him in the Holy Ghost, constitute His mystical body, and that if any member of that body is in a suffering condition, the head shares all the phenomena of pain or pleasure, which any member of the body may undergo. Hence we are told that in all our afflictions Jesus is afflicted.

When Saul of Tarsus was galloping to Damascus to torture the little flock of believers, he was arrested by the Head of the Church, who said, "Saul, Saul, why persecuteth thou me?" Jesus identified the humble saints in Damascus with Himself, as our head feels the torture of any of our bodily members. Saul thought he was crushing out some fanatics, but those fanatics turned out to be the vital members of the eternal Christ enthroned at the right hand of God. This same thing has been repeated thousands of times, and is still transpiring in many parts of the earth. The humble and despised ones, who are in many instances looked upon as irregular cranks and unmanageable extremists in religion, are the members of the living Christ, and He still comes down in spirit and enters into every infinitesimal detail of their private lives. We have never yet half believed all that the Scriptures teach us concerning that perfect measure with which Jesus identifies us with Himself. If we are living in blessed obedience to Him and trusting Him alone and fully on all lines, He makes every single interest of our whole being and life to be His own. He feels every pain that we have, whether physical or mental or spiritual. He in spirit weeps with us when we weep, and prays with us when we pray, and suffers with us when we suffer.

The Holy Spirit is in the divine realm what our nervous system is in our bodies, and with infinitely more accuracy and certainty than our nerves can transmit a sensation from our extremities to the brain, the Holy Spirit, as the divine nerve, transmits every variety and every degree of sensation in the believer to His divine Head, the blessed Jesus. This is the purport of the promise, "I will sup with him." To sup with a person means to share with them what they may have, whether good or bad, joyful or sorrowful; the poor crust and a cup of water, or the feast of fat things. Hence Christ supping with us not only implies His inevitable and personal participation and consciousness with all our temptations, and tears, and struggles, but also that He just as consciously and as directly participates in all our joys. He is happy in our happiness, and smiles with our smiles, and has a pleasure in every pure and innocent joy of His children, and rejoices in His spirit at every step they take in Christian progress. When on the earth He affirmed that He rejoiced in spirit at the downfall of Satan, but if that was a source of joy to His immaculate heart, how much more so does He rejoice in our new birth, and our sanctification, and every act of our loving obedience and trust to Him?

This participation of Jesus of the love of His disciples is set forth in the Song of Solomon in these words, "My beloved is mine, and I am his. He feedeth among the lilies." Several times the expression is used that Christ feeds among the lilies, and goes down into His garden to smell the fragrant blossoms and the spices. The lily is a Scripture type of a purified believer, whose white, clean heart gives forth in its love, and faith, and hope, and obedience, and heavenly aspirations, those sweet perfumes which are more fragrant to Jesus than all the odors of spicy Arabia. We are told in the Scripture that the prayers of the saints smell sweet to God, and they are emblematized as sweet incense of burning spices.

Love always feeds upon love, and the heart of love has a mystical way of feeding itself just as truly as the body has of taking nourishment. When a mother sits by her sleeping babe, engaged in her daily work, and ever and anon fixes her soft, maternal gaze upon her little darling, could we see the interior mechanism of her soul, thoughts, and affections, we would discover that her loving heart was feeding on that babe in a mystical way just as really as the fish feed on the sea, or as the mind feeds on books, or as the body feeds on bread. In like manner Jesus bends over those who love Him with a perfect heart. He enjoys their prayers, their songs, their testimonies, their unselfish and loving efforts to promote His glory. Every loyal thought that we have toward Him, every desire we have to see Him, and to serve Him, every sacrifice we make to extend His salvation among men, is a little banquet to His infinite heart. And all this is transpiring, and so few of us ever take into our thoughtful appreciation even a small tithe of His personal, profound, and perpetual interest in us. Could we see all this as we shall see it some day, how it would invigorate our love, and fortify our zeal, and relieve our loneliness, and make our very hearts flutter with a bewildering sense of His dear presence in us and with us every moment of our lives. O, why is it that we do not believe Him more, and then surely we would love Him more. If we in reality perfectly apprehend the truth of His words, "Lo I am with you all the days, even to the end of the age," how that living faith would transform our inner and outer lives, and beget within us that habit of recollection and of practicing the presence of God, which would throw the very luster of heaven upon our spirit and our behavior. And yet He is true to His own word, and whether we fully apprehend it or not. He does sup with us if we sincerely throw the door of our hearts open to Him for His unreserved possession.

Chapter XIV
"HE WILL SUP WITH ME"
Rev. 3:20

JUST AS TRULY as Jesus comes down in spirit to sup with those who fully admit Him into their hearts, so they will be taken up at His second coming, and sup with Him in that banquet, of which He has told us in His parables and through the lips of His apostles. The special promise connected with the seventh overcometh is that of sitting with Jesus in His millennial throne; but before that throne is actually set up on this earth there must intervene that great crisis which is referred to in the 20th verse of this third chapter of Revelation, namely: that of sitting with Jesus at the marriage supper of the Lamb. If we compile all the various events which will be concomitant with the coming of Christ in the clouds of heaven we find them to comprise the following items: The Lord Jesus will descend from the right hand of the Father, accompanied by tens of thousands of angels and saints. He will be preceded by the archangel, who will blow the trumpet of God for the first resurrection. Those sainted dead who during their life in the flesh were regenerated, and sanctified, and sufficiently tried to constitute them martyrs in spirit will be raised from the dead, and glorified, and taken up in the air to meet Jesus. Also those Christians on earth who are entirely yielded to God, and whose hearts have been purified and filled with the Holy Spirit, constituting them the five wise virgins, who have oil in their vessels, will be suddenly glorified and caught up in the clouds with those of the first resurrection to meet the Lord. (Compare I. Thess. 4, and Revelation 20.) When Jesus thus appears in the clouds of glory, He will not put His foot on this earth at that time, for He tells us He will come as a flash of lightning from the east to the west, and encircle the entire globe, and gather out His elect ones from the four winds of heaven, or as it is distinctly prophesied in Psalms 50: "Our God shall come, and He shall call to the heavens, and the earth, that He may judge His people." The word "judge" here does not mean to condemn, but to discriminate, or discern who His people are, and He will then say: "Gather my saints together unto me, those who have made a covenant with me by sacrifice." This is an express declaration that only those who are really saints, and who have made a covenant by the complete sacrifice of themselves to God, shall be gathered up. At the same time we are told that all nations and kindred shall wail because of Him, and again, that people will run in perfect consternation to hide themselves in dens and caves of the earth.

After Jesus has taken away His elect ones, God the Father, as the Ancient of Days in Daniel, will institute the great judgment tribulations on the world for having rejected Jesus, and on the fallen churches for having rejected the baptism of the Holy Ghost. Those awful tribulations are described by Jeremiah, 25th chapter, and by Ezekiel in the 38th chapter, and by St. John in Revelation, chapter 18 and chapter 19:17 to 21, and in a great many other places in Scripture. While these tribulations are taking place in all the earth, Jesus and His elect saints, who have been resurrected or translated, will be in some heavenly place, which is described in Psalms 45 as "ivory palaces," and partake of that divine banquet, which is prophesied in the parable of the king's wedding, and in the Song of Solomon and in Revelation 19. Concerning this supper we will notice:

1. That it is emphatically a supper of the perfected and then glorified believers with Jesus. Now just as truly, and perfectly, and minutely as Jesus comes down in spirit to sup with His saints here, and enters into all the details and experiences of their lives, so, on the other hand, the glorified saints, in supping with Jesus, will ascend up into His glory, and be admitted into every secret of His glorious personality, and life, and kingdom, and joy, and honor, and be made to participate in every variety of His bliss, and every detail of His glory, and every majesty of His kingdom. What little we have learned of Jesus is simply of His humiliation, and suffering, and death; that is, Jesus in His prophetic and priestly offices, but we have scarcely begun to learn anything of Him as a king in the royalty of His royal majesty and those manifold and uncreated glories that the Father has given to Him. Just so truly as Jesus now comes to us in spirit, so truly will we who are prepared go to Him in a body. Just as truly as He comes to us now invisibly, we shall go to Him visibly. Just as truly as He now consciously feels our sorrows and pains, just so truly we shall then consciously enter into His bliss and the manifold departments of His joy and glory. Just as truly as He now identifies Himself with His suffering saints, speaking of them as a part of Himself, so truly at that day the saints will realize that Jesus is one with them,

that His glory is their glory, His bliss their bliss, His real majesty their own majesty, His rights as the ruler of the world their own rights. We have no thoughts to think these things, and no words adequate to express them. What will it be to enter into the joy of our Lord, and yet that is the exact promise. The joys of Jesus are manifold. It is an eternal joy for Him to be the only begotten Son of the Father. It is another joy to be the second Adam, the only pure man that never had sin. It is another joy to be the redeemer of sinful men, and to love them to the death. It is another joy to be the head of the church, the shepherd of God's sheep. It is another joy to be the giver of the blessed Holy Ghost, to sanctify and fill the breast of His mystical body. It is another joy to be the Creator of all worlds and all beings, to be the architect of every grain of sand, every insect, every living creature, and every bright star that glitters in its orbit. It is another joy to be the only person in the universe who is the revealer of the Eternal Father, and the outspoken word from the bosom of that Father. It is another joy for Him to sit in judgment on the human race, and deal out to each creature his exact reward with perfect justice. It is another joy that He wears upon His head many crowns as the appointed and only sovereign of the three empires of nature, grace, and glory, and to govern the worlds, and all angels, and all men in absolute goodness and equity. It is another joy that He is to come back to this earth, where He had His human birth, and from whose dust His precious body was formed, and where He shed His precious blood, and to govern this earth in His humanity as the Son of Man. These are only a few of the many joys that concenter and unite in the soul of Jesus, and make that soul to be a white furnace of inexpressible bliss. And yet into all these joys which we can feebly think of, and others that we cannot imagine, we are to enter if we are prepared.

This is what it will be to sup with Jesus, to share all His

fullness and estates just as fully, beautifully, tenderly, and consciously as a bride can share the joys and estates and sovereignty of her husband, who is the king over a great empire. Could we but get a glimpse of heaven, a small fraction of what it will be to sup with Jesus, we should almost be beside ourselves with holy love and flaming zeal in His service here.

2. We are fully warranted from many passages in Scripture in believing that in heaven, in the glorified state, we shall still have some kind of created nourishment. Many persons have formed unnatural and unscriptural notions of the heavenly state as being diametrically opposed to everything in the present state of existence. But such should not be the case. Those persons who deny the literal resurrection of the body, do so from a foolish and unscriptural fancy that matter in and of itself, is too degraded to exist in a glorified manner. But matter of itself is not sinful, and the three persons of the Godhead walked and communed with Adam and Eve before their fall in a literal and material world, and their literal bodies of flesh and blood, and their feeding literally on the fruit of the trees, did not in the least hinder this world from being at that time a part of heaven, nor hindered in the least their fellowship with angels and with God, and to suppose that after we are glorified we shall no longer need any form of created nourishment is both unphilosophical and unscriptural. The Lord Jesus and two angels visited Abraham just before the destruction of Sodom and Gomorrah, and the patriarch entertained them, and cooked for them a dinner, of which they partook. It is expressly declared in Scripture that when God fed the Israelites with manna from heaven that "He gave them angels' food to eat." If this Scripture does not mean exactly what it says, what can it mean? God does not mock us with hypocritical lan-

guage, and to whittle such Scriptures away into a mere
ghostly metaphor is the very essence of unbelief, which
sets up the human reason as being wiser than the infallible statements of the Holy Spirit. The angels live
on some kind of created diet like the manna.

After Moses led the Israelites out of Egypt to Mt. Sinai,
we are told that he and the seventy elders went up into
Mt. Horeb, and they saw the God of Israel, and there
was under His feet a paved work of the sapphire stone,
and also they saw God, and did eat and drink. (Ex. 24.)
This is a prophetic type of the glorified saints, after being
taken out of the world, as the Jews were taken out of
Egypt, going up into the Mountains of the Lord, and
having the beatific vision of God, and eating and drinking with the Lord Jesus in His heavenly kingdom.

"When Jesus instituted the Lord's supper, after eating
the roast lamb and bread, He took the cup and gave it to
the eleven disciples (for Judas had left), and said, "This is
my blood of the New Testament, but I will not drink
henceforth of the fruit of the vine until that day when I
drink it new with you in my Father's kingdom." It is
worse than trifling to twist these words of Jesus into a
mere mythical meaning. We see here that Judas left before this cup was passed around, and only those were
present who were the real elect. So only those will sup
with Jesus in His coming banquet, who are the real holy
and tried ones. The cup of wine that Jesus gave to His
disciples was not mythical, nor imaginary wine, but the
real fruit of the vine; and, just as literally as that was the
fruit of the vine, Jesus affirms that He will drink of the
real fruit of the vine with His saints in that day in His
Father's kingdom. Hence the one wine is just as real as
the other. (Matt. 26.) Again, St. Luke reports the words
of Jesus, that those disciples who continue with Christ in
His temptations, He says to such, "I appoint unto you a
kingdom, as my Father has appointed unto me, that ye

may eat and drink at my table, in my kingdom, and sit on thrones, judging the twelve tribes of Israel." (Luke 22.) These words mean exactly what they say. That just as really as God the Father has appointed Jesus to the kingdom, Jesus in turn appoints His elect saints to be every one of them princes and princesses, and to have rulership in a real literal government. And He says, without any equivocation, that these elect ones shall eat and drink at His table. These words will be fulfilled at the marriage supper of the Lamb, and then this supper will be followed by these elect saints sitting on thrones and judging and governing the twelve tribes of Israel; that is, the apostles will come back from the wedding, and all the twelve tribes will be restored to Palestine in the millennial age, and accept the Christ as their Messiah, and these twelve tribes will be governed by the glorified apostles and saints. And so the promise made in the first overcometh concerning the eating of the tree of life will have just as real a fulfillment as Adam and Eve partook of the fruit in the garden of Eden. Because the Scripture has a spiritual application that does not hinder it from having an outward and a literal fulfillment.

3. Another class of events which will transpire at the marriage supper of the Lamb will be the judging of the members who comprise the bridehood, and the giving to each one of them their rewards, and assigning to each one of those glorified millions, who are typified by the hundred and forty-four thousand, their respective places in that glorious army, that living city. That will be the time when all the living stones which have been quarried from the mines of earth, and fashioned by divine grace, will be silently and sweetly knit together, to make up the radiant whole, of which the building of the temple by King Solomon was a prophetic emblem. King David is a type of Jesus in His humiliation and suffering, and King Solomon is a type of Jesus in His millennial reign on earth.

And as King David, before his death, prepared the material for the building of the temple, and then Solomon took the material and built the structure, so in like manner Jesus, in His humiliation, sufferings and death, and through the patient operation of the Holy Ghost in this present age, has been preparing the material for the structure of the New Jerusalem, then Jesus in His second coming, and at His marriage banquet, will carry out the typology of King Solomon, and there form into a gorgeous structure the living souls that make the city, which is like pure gold and shining with the glory of God. We have another type of this city formation in the acts of Moses, who, after bringing the Israelites out of Egypt to Mt. Sinai, there formed them into a living city, and arranged them according to a divine pattern, putting three tribes on the north, three on the east, three on the south, and three on the west, giving to each tribe, and family, and individual, his exact place in that beautiful portable city, according to the mind of God, and in the hollow square he placed the glorious tabernacle, upon which rested the pillar of cloud by day and the pillar of fire by night. That transaction, we are told, was according to the pattern of things in heaven, and it had a meaning infinitely beyond the time then present, and stretched away across the centuries to that crowning historical event of the gathering out of the true Israel from the Egypt of this present world, and forming them each one from the different nations and the different centuries in his exact place in the divine city, where each of God's saints will find his proper place as accurately as each bone in the body has its appropriate fitting of bone with bone, and part with part. It is a vision of that living city of glorified saints that John described in Revelation 21. Each of those twelve precious stones will have their counterpart in a twelvefold variety of holy character.

If the reader will turn to the 19th chapter of Revelation, he will notice in the first part of the chapter an account of this marriage supper of the Lamb, and while that is taking place up in the heavenly places, in the latter part of the chapter will be found the description of the great supper of the wrath of God which is taking place among the nations on the earth. The word "sun," in verse 17, symbolizes royalty, or heads of government, and an angel will move all the kings and heads of government into a declaration of war. The "fowls" referred to always signify demons, and these demons take delight in bloodshed and war. A battlefield is the devil's revival, and his supper table, and so, when captains, and kings, and horses, and soldiers are being slaughtered in war, the devils have their banquet. Thus we see clearly that while in verse 9 Jesus and His saints are having the wedding supper in the air, the whole earth is in a state of carnage and suffering in the great tribulations as described in verses 17 to 20.

If we expect to be admitted to the marriage of the Lamb we must be arrayed in fine linen, clean and glistening, as the Greek puts it, for the fine linen is the righteousness of saints, and blessed are they which are called unto the marriage supper of the Lamb.

As to the length of time which the great tribulations will last, and the coetaneous time occupied by the marriage supper, from all the best data we can gather, it will be about forty years. Some have supposed that two and one-half years, and others have thought that seven years, will be the length of time for these events, but I am convinced that they will occupy about the period of forty years. If we examine the time set forth in the last chapter of Daniel, and deduct the prophetic day—year—of the time for the treading down of Jerusalem to the opening of the new age, it leaves between thirty-five and forty years for the great tribulations and the heavenly banquet.

Noah's flood is a perfect type of the second coming of Christ and concomitant events. We are told that after Noah and his family went up into the ark, "that it rained forty days and nights." The ascent of Noah in the ark represents the ascent of the translated ones in the air, and the forty days of rain represent the forty years of tribulation, as we are told, both by Moses and Ezekiel, that a day in prophecy stands for a year. And then when the flood began to subside, we are told, that from the time the ark rested on Mt. Ararat, that Noah waited forty days, and then sent forth the dove. So both at the beginning of the flood, and at its drying up, we have a forty year emblem. As far as we can cipher out the time of the ten plagues, which were sent on the Egyptians, they covered the space of forty days. That is another emblem of the forty years of tribulation on the whole earth. In the 29th chapter of Ezekiel, he prophesies the utter desolation of the land of Egypt, and says the land should "not be inhabited forty years," which is another prophetic type of the desolations in all the earth, after the saints are taken out. We know that the number forty in Scripture always signifies the period for punishing, proving, trying, and testing a person, or nation, or thing. From the time Jesus was born until He ascended to heaven, covered the duration of one generation of thirty-three years. During that time there was the winding up of the Jewish age, and the opening up of the Christian Gentile age; and so it would seem, that in the transition period, from the close of the present Gentile age to the opening of the new millennial age, there will again be about the space of one generation.

After the Hebrews left Egypt, and reached Mt. Horeb, Moses went up into the mountain and spent forty days and nights with God, which is a clear and beautiful type, that after the saints leave this earth they will spend forty years with God in the upper regions of the air. As Moses after forty days descended from the mountain top with his face radiant with the glory of God, to be the lawgiver and leader of the armies of God, in like manner, the elect saints, after spending forty years with Jesus at His heavenly banquet, will return back to this earth filled with the radiant glory of God; and, as Jesus says, they will shine like the sun in His kingdom, and at that time they will, under Christ, take charge as judges, leaders, rulers, and teachers, of all the nations of the earth. Hence it would seem, from all these analogies, that the marriage supper of the Lamb, and the great tribulations, will extend through the period of forty years.

Chapter XV
"In My Throne"
Rev. 3:21

WE HAVE NOW COME to the last of the seven overcomeths, which brings us up to the period just after supping with Jesus on high and the setting up of His theocratic throne in the earth. "To him that overcometh will I grant to sit with me in my throne, even as I also overcame and am set down with my Father in His throne." To take an explicit promise like this, and confine it only to a mystical and spiritual significance, is to do great violence to the word of God. We know that a "throne" is the head and center of a government, of a kingdom, and to sit in a throne means to occupy the place of royalty and share the supreme authority, and unless Jesus has a real literal kingdom of His own, and unless He is going to receive His perfectly loyal followers into participation with Him in the dominion and rulership in that kingdom, then there are scores of passages of Scripture which are utterly meaningless. In the book of Daniel we have a description of four great kingdoms that should arise in the earth, and then a description of the kingdom of the Son of Man, which should break in pieces all the other kingdoms, as a stone cut out of the mountain without hands.

Now, if the kingdom of the Son of Man is merely mystical, then the other four kingdoms are merely mystical also, and on the other hand, if the four kingdoms described by Daniel were real, veritable kingdoms on this earth, then with the same absolute certainty the kingdom of the Lord Jesus will be real and veritable upon this earth. The one is no more mythical than is the other. In looking into this promise of sitting with Christ in His throne, let us consider the following items:

1. The Scriptures nowhere tell us that the Lord Jesus has yet occupied His own throne. This may startle some at first, but let the Word of God settle it. The eternal Son of God is equal with the Father in nature, and substance, and attributes. But let us remember that God the Father has given to His Son Jesus, as a God-Man, as the Son of Man, and as the Savior of Men, a distinct throne and government over man and over this earth. Now all the Scriptures which speak of Jesus ascending on high represent Him as sitting "with the Father on the Father's throne," and "at the right hand of the Father," as a "mediator between God and man," but not one of these Scriptures speak of Jesus being on His own throne as the Son of Man. We read in the 7th chapter of Acts that when Stephen was being stoned to death he looked up into heaven and saw the glory of God, and Jesus standing on the right hand of God, and he said: "I see the heavens opened and the Son of Man standing on the right hand of God." Here there is no vision of Jesus being on His Messianic throne, but of His being at the right hand of the Father's throne.

In the second chapter of Acts, Peter is expounding the Messiahship of Jesus as the lineal son and heir of King

David, and quotes that Psalm where the Lord said to Jesus: "Sit thou on my right hand, until I make thy enemies thy footstool." God the Father has promised to conquer the enemies of Jesus, and especially to subdue and bring back to Christ the twelve tribes of Israel. This the Father will do in His judgment as the Ancient of Days, in the great tribulations He will make the nations of the earth, and especially the descendants of Abraham, so humble that they will gladly welcome Jesus back from the wedding, and be His footstool for His millennial kingdom. At that time Jesus will ascend His own throne as King of the World and Messiah of the twelve tribes. But during the interval between the ascension of Christ from Mt. Olivet to His second coming, Jesus is on the Father's throne, interceding for His people, and awaiting the hour to take His own throne.

In the third chapter of Colossians the believer' is represented as rising from the death of sin, and seeking with all his heart those things which are above, "where Christ sitteth on the right hand of God." Here there is no allusion to Christ being on His own throne, but on the Father's throne. We read in the ninth chapter of Hebrews that Christ has entered into the holy of holies in heaven, "to appear in the presence of God for us." We again read that He is "at the right hand of the Majesty on high," and again that He is on the throne of grace, that is, of merciful intercession, where He can bestow the gifts of repentance, and saving faith, and salvation. But in none of these Scriptures do we get the representation of Jesus being on His own individual throne as a glorified man to govern the world.

2. When we come to search into all those numerous passages that set forth Jesus as a ruler and a king over the nations, we learn that He, as a glorified man, has been appointed of God the Father to rule this world. Just as literally as God made Adam and Eve to be a king and

queen, and to have dominion over everything on this earth, so Jesus, as the second Adam and the heir of David, is to own and govern this world, not merely as an eternal person of the Godhead, but as an incarnate God, as a perfectly holy and obedient man, as the son of Mary and the son of David, He is to rule this world. In His divinity as the Creator of All Worlds, He owns this globe, but in His humanity, here is where His body was prepared for Him, out of the dust of this planet. Here is where He was born of a human mother and had His temporal generation. This earth has been moistened with His tears and baptized with His blood, and He as a Man has absolute rights over this planet, and over all its population, in a manner different from His rights over any other material world. This line of thought is often utterly omitted when people read the Scriptures concerning the kingdom of Jesus.

David was the founder of God's theocratic government among men. He was a man and a king after God's own heart, and the Lord made an eternal covenant with David, that of the seed of His flesh He would raise up a king that should govern this world forever and ever. Jesus was, in His human nature, the lineal offspring of King David, and is to occupy David's throne, and enlarge, and perfect, and establish, that theocratic government, which was started in the reign of King David. Hence Jesus is compared to David, far more than to any and all other men in the Bible, and His kingdom as a glorified man is so frequently termed "the kingdom of David," and His throne as a son of man, is often called "the throne of David." In the third chapter of Hosea, we read the prophecy of the kingdom of Israel going into eclipse, until the millennial reign of Jesus. "For the children of Israel shall abide many days without a king, and without a prince, and without a sacrifice." These words are literally fulfilled in the cessation of the Jewish government, which has now lasted nearly thirteen centuries. "Afterward shall the children of Israel return, and seek the Lord their God, and David their King, and shall fear the Lord and His goodness in the latter days." Here is a specific promise of the return of the twelve tribes of Israel to the Lord in the latter days, that is, in the millennium, and then Jesus, who is here called David, will be their king, and they will love and serve Him throughout His millennial reign. Language could hardly be more definite than this prophecy, and that language has not yet been fulfilled. We read in the 30th chapter of Jeremiah of the time when the people of "Israel shall return to the Lord, and to David their king, and that at that time their King David which is Jesus, shall save them from afar, and Jacob shall return, and shall be in rest, and be quiet, and none shall make him afraid."

The prophecies of Isaiah, Jeremiah, and Ezekiel, contain many descriptions of the theocratic reign of the Lord Jesus on this earth, as King David, or as the Son of David. To deny the literal fulfillment of these prophecies is to convert the Word of God into Swedenborgian mysticism, and do violence to all the rules of scriptural interpretation.

In the 34th chapter of Ezekiel, we have a most exact and beautiful portrayal of the reign of the Lord on this earth, under the name of David, at which time, "He will make with all nations a covenant of peace, and will cause evil beasts to cease out of the land, and the people shall dwell safely in the wilderness, and sleep in the woods," and at that time He will make the trees of the field yield their fruit, and make the earth to yield her increase, and everything shall be safe in the land, and this King David shall break the bands of every yoke, and be at that time a plant of renown. If these words do not mean exactly what they say, then prophecy is a mere myth. In the first chapter of the Gospel by Luke, the angel Gabriel, who announced to Mary the birth of Jesus, told her expressly, "that her son Jesus should be great, and should be called the Son of the Highest, and that the Lord God should give unto Him the throne of His Father David, and that He should reign over the house of Jacob forever, and that of His kingdom there should be no end." Now remember, that these words of the angel Gabriel were addressed to Mary as the Mother of Jesus, and they prophesy the throne that Jesus should have as a man, and as the royal heir of King David. Jesus has never yet ruled over the twelve tribes of Jacob, as their own king, and so this prophecy has not yet been fulfilled, but it is to have an exact and literal accomplishment.

If we notice the parables of Jesus concerning His second coming, He so often says that at that time "the Son of Man shall sit in the throne of His glory," and at the same time those who have followed Him fully shall be glorified and sit with Him on thrones, judging the twelve tribes of Israel." (Matt. 19:27, 28.) And again, He speaks of "the Son of Man coming in His kingdom." He says that "when the Son of Man shall come in His glory, that then He shall sit upon the throne of His glory." (Matt. 25:31.) Jesus never speaks of sitting on His throne in His glory except in connection with His second coming.

Thus we see, from a great number of Scriptures, the theocratic throne of David is to be restored and established in a literal government over all the nations of this world. In harmony with this line of exposition, we see in the 19th chapter of Revelation an account of "the Lamb's wife making herself ready, and being arrayed in fine linen, and then of her being called to the marriage supper of the Lamb; and this is followed by a glorious description of the Lord Jesus, with eyes as a flame of fire, and on His head many crowns, and being clothed in a vesture dipped in blood, and the armies in heaven, that is, the glorified members of His bridehood, following him, riding upon white horses, and this is followed by His taking charge of all the nations, and smiting the refractory elements of society as with a rod of iron, and then of His assuming the title of King of kings and Lord of lords."

Thus we see that each verse presents a successive unfolding of consecutive events which are concurrent with the marriage supper, and immediately following that supper. This is the same line of truth presented in the closing verses of this third chapter of Revelation, where the translated saints and the resurrection saints are to sup with Jesus, and this is followed by Christ assuming the throne of David, and re-establishing the theocratic kingdom on earth, and then taking the glorified members of His bridehood into partnership with Himself, and giving them places in His government as sitting with Him on the throne. It is in the light of this interpretation that we are to understand that large class of Scriptures which set forth that "if we suffer with Him we shall also reign with Him." But let us remember that the word suffer in this connection does not mean any kind of suffering, but it is the same word which is used of the crucifixion of Jesus, that is, "if we are crucified with Him we shall reign with Him." There is not a single text of Scripture which represents the new birth of itself as qualifying any one to reign with Christ in His coming kingdom, but in every single place where reigning with Christ is spoken of there are terms used which indicate something more than justification, terms strongly expressive of being dead to sin, of following Christ to the death, of being purified, made white, and tried.

3. Now Christ affirms that those who are the overcomers will share His coming kingdom just as emphatically and as surely as He at the present time as a glorified man is sharing the Father's government in heaven. Jesus tells

us in this 21st verse that He has overcome, and is now sitting down with the Father in the Father's throne, and just as much as that is a literal fact, so He affirms that His perfectly loyal disciples, shall sit in His government when He reigns on the earth.

In a vast empire there are a great many departments of government. When we look into the structure of the Kingdom of Great Britain or the United States we find a great many departments of government and each of the heads of these various departments have under them officers and assistants, divided and subdivided, extending into ramified details, covering the whole territory of government in its legislative and judicial and executive functions, at home and abroad, in its commercial, educational, religious, agricultural, scientific, and social relations, furnishing busy employment and a field for the exercise of innumerable gifts and capabilities to many thousands of persons. Thus when the Lord Jesus, as a glorified man and the crowned heir of David, shall sit on His throne as the King of this World, He will institute the greatest and most glorious and most diversified empire ever known to the human mind. All the kings that have ever existed in this world in their most perfect state of glory will be in comparison with the theocratic Kingdom of Jesus only as a feeble glowworm to the splendor of a noonday summer sun. Jesus Himself speaks of Himself and His glorified disciples "as shining like the sun in that kingdom."

We are told by the prophet Daniel that during the great tribulations under the judgments of the Ancient of Days, "that the thrones of the earth will be cast down," that is, every human government on this earth will go to wreck in those tribulations, and all the ecclesiastical organization of the fallen churches will crumble to pieces, all secret societies and corporate organizations and federated associations will at that time crumble to pieces, and when Jesus "returns from the wedding to take His kingdom,"

He will find the people on the earth in a state of practical anarchy and governmental dissolution. It will be out of the wreck of all these forms of government that Jesus will organize His kingdom and remodel the geography of the globe and appoint to each member of His glorified bridehood an appropriate office of service and a principality of honor in that kingdom. These various principalities are more distinctly set forth in the 4th chapter of Revelation which we are to hereafter consider.

Chapter XVI
"THE RAINBOW AROUND THE THRONE"
Rev. 4:3

IN UNDERSTANDING THE BOOK of Revelation we must remember that, while it is in some sense a consecutive unveiling of historical events, from the days of St. John to the end of the Christian age, and the end of the millennium at the same time, the visions are given in different sections, so that in some respects the same historical ground is repeated over again. As for instance the first four chapters is a setting forth of events from the days of John up to the millennial kingdom with especial reference to stages of the visible church. Then another series of visions is given with reference to the political history of the nations, such as the rise of popery and Mohammedism. Then another series of visions with reference to God's judgments upon the nations, the downfall of Romanism, and the great tribulations.

As we now come to the fourth chapter of Revelation, we have here the setting up of Christ's theocratic throne in the Kingdom of God on this earth. Hence the events prophesied in this chapter occur immediately after the marriage supper of the Lamb. As it is said in the first verse of this chapter: "Come up hither, and I will show thee the things which must be hereafter" — that is, such as will take place immediately after the things which are prophesied in the close of the third chapter. Then John says: "I beheld, and a throne was set up in heaven." Let us remember our key of interpretation in the first chapter, that this word "heaven" means the Kingdom of God on earth. This throne does not mean the eternal throne of the triune Godhead, for that we know was set up from all eternity, and neither John nor any angel saw when it was instituted. But this throne is surely that of David, which belongs to Jesus Christ as David's son, as the King of the Jews, as the Redeemer and heir of the world, and this throne, which is another word for the theocratic government, will be set up on this earth, when Jesus and His glorified bridehood return from the wedding, after the great tribulations, and immediately after the chaining and binding of Satan, which is described in the twentieth chapter, You will notice that in the twentieth chapter the angel is sent to bind Satan, and shut him up a thousand years, and the next verse says that there were thrones set up, which are the thrones to be occupied by the glorified saints, who are to share the government with Jesus, and on these thrones were placed those martyrs, or those entirely devoted saints who had in them in this life the martyr spirit for Jesus, and it is expressly said "that they shall live and reign with Christ a thousand years."

Now this throne spoken of in the fourth chapter, surrounded by the rainbow, and filled with the living creatures, is the instituting of the millennial government over the nations.

1. It is clearly set forth in Scripture that this millennial throne will be set up in Jerusalem. Perhaps it is not sufficiently understood that Palestine is the very heart of the world, and just about the center of the globe geographi-

cally, and with reference to the world's population. So much so that if all human beings were compelled by some stern necessity to assemble at any one given spot on the earth, they could all meet at Palestine easier and quicker than at any other place on earth. Moses tells us that when the Most High divided to all the nations of the world their several inheritance, and when He separated the sons of Adam into their nationalities, that He set the boundaries of the people, that is, their geographical limits, according to the number of the children of Israel. (Deut. 32.) From this I learn that God constituted the twelve tribes of Israel, the very historical center of all the nations of mankind, and gave them the Land of Canaan, which is the geographical center of the globe. This fact has a marvelous significance, which perhaps few of us have ever apprehended. The Land of Canaan is a miniature world in itself, embracing within the narrow limits of one hundred and fifty miles one way, by fifty and seventy-five miles the other, all the climates of the world, from ever-lasting snow to everlasting summer, and all the products of the world. So that it is a miniature world, and is to have a history in the coming age more marvelous than anything in former ages, in which the extraordinary prophecies of Scripture will be fulfilled.

There are prophecies in the 33d chapter of Isaiah, concerning Zion and Jerusalem, which have never been fulfilled, and which have more than a mere spiritual application, for it is Zion and the City of Jerusalem which is to be a quiet habitation, and never taken down, and never removed, and it is there that the Lord will reveal Himself. There are to be rivers and streams, upon which there are no galley slave boats, or war ships, but where the King shall be seen in His beauty, and where the lame shall take the prey, and where the inhabitant shall not say he is sick.

We are told in the 3d chapter of Jeremiah, of the return

of the backsliding Israel, and "at that time we shall call Jerusalem the throne of the Lord, and all the nations shall be gathered into it, to the name of the Lord, to Jerusalem." That prophecy has never yet been fulfilled, but will receive its perfect fulfillment when Jesus returns from the wedding, and sets up His theocratic government as the throne of David in Jerusalem, and then literally all the nations of the earth will be, by their representatives, gathered to Jerusalem. This will be the time when the prophecy in the 14th of Revelation will be fulfilled, where John says, "I looked, and lo, a Lamb stood on the Mount Zion, and with Him an hundred and forty and four thousand, having His Father's name written in their foreheads." Here we see again, that the setting up of Christ's millennial government, is accompanied by that special number of glorified saints who compose the bride of the Lamb, "and who were the first fruits redeemed from among the nations, and who follow the Lamb whithersoever He goeth." We are told in the Apocrypha, that when the Lord shall reign on the earth in His glory, that the City of Jerusalem should be rebuilt with sapphires and diamonds, and it is very probable that God has vast mines of sapphires and diamonds, hid away in some mountain range, which He will not let any one discover until that time.

2. "He that sat upon the throne was to look upon, like a jasper and the sardius." This is a vision of the inexpressible beauty and glory of Jesus as He will appear to His saints and the people of the earth in His millennial kingdom. This is like the vision of Him which Daniel had, and which John describes in the first chapter of Revelation. The "jasper" is the precious stone which is the wall of the heavenly Jerusalem, and the sardine, the same as sardius, or a blood red ruby, is the center stone in the heavenly city; hence we see that Jesus unites in Himself every glory from the center to the circumference of the City of God, and every possible gift, and grace, and maj-

esty, and charm which it is possible for the Godhead to bestow upon the humanity of the Incarnate Word.

As Jesus, after the resurrection, appeared and disappeared at will to His servants, appointing them a place to meet, and suddenly appearing in their midst and holding sweet communion with them, and then vanishing out of their sight, so it will be when He reigns on this earth.

3. "There was a rainbow round about the throne, in sight like unto an emerald." This rainbow, the predominant color of which was green, opens up a vast range of glorious things which will exist in the millennial kingdom. This is a companion picture in all respects with that which is set forth in the 9th chapter of Genesis, when God stretched the rainbow over Noah's altar, just after the flood. Jesus Himself tells us, in the 24th chapter of Matthew, of the wonderful analogy between Noah's flood and His second coming, and that analogy is more accurate and marvelous than we might at first sight apprehend. The ascent of Noah and his family up into the ark corresponds with the ascent of those in the first resurrection and the translated saints into the air to meet Jesus. The descent of the rain punishing the inhabitants living in sin corresponds with the great tribulations. The return of the ark with its inhabitants back to Mount Ararat corresponds with the return of Jesus and His glorified saints back to Mount Zion, at which time, Zechariah tells us, Jesus will put his foot on Mount Olivet. The going forth of Noah and his sons to take charge of the new world beautifully represents the going forth of Jesus and His hundred and forty-four thousand to take charge of the world in the millennial age. The altar erected by Noah, on which to offer sacrifices, corresponds with the theocratic throne erected for Jesus at the opening of the new age. The rainbow over Noah's altar, as a sign of God's covenant, corresponds with the rainbow around the millennial throne of Jesus, as the pledge of the millennial covenant, and the

fulfilling of all the prophecies, and the bringing in of everlasting righteousness, and the filling of the earth with
the glory of the Lord as the waters cover the sea. Everything in the Old Testament has a companion piece in the
New Testament, and the 9th of Genesis and the 4th of
Revelation are companion chapters, the one being the
fulfillment of the other. Isaiah prophesied of this millennial
kingdom, with its rainbow at the opening of the new age
or divine glory on earth.

If we carefully read Isaiah 54th we will see a description of the Lord as a Husband being married to believers
that should be selected from among the Gentiles, and that
the Lord, under the character of a Husband and a Redeemer, shall be called in that day the God of the whole
earth, and that He will establish His everlasting kindness,
and that the curse which He put on the earth should be
removed just as the waters of Noah's flood were removed,
and that the covenant which He made with Noah concerning the earth not being drowned any more should
be repeated and refulfilled in the covenant of peace which
He will make at that time. He also prophesies the building up of His millennial throne and kingdom in Jerusalem by laying the foundations with sapphires, and making the windows of agates and the gates of rubies, and
that righteousness shall be established, and ail terror and
fear removed, and concludes the gorgeous prophecy by
saying, "This is the heritage of the servants of the Lord."
Thus Isaiah prophesies the intimate connection between
the facts and phenomena of Noah opening the new age
and Jesus opening the millennial age.

4. There is great significance in the fact that the predominant color in the rainbow was that of emerald or
green. This color represents hope, verdure, or spring of
the year, prosperity. When the High Priest in the Jewish
economy put on his breastplate, there were twelve precious stones in the breastplate, a stone for each of the

twelve tribes, and it is significant that the stone for Judah was that of the emerald. God foresaw that Judah was to be the ruling tribe, from which should spring King David and his greater Son, King Jesus. Hence God selected the emerald as the precious gem of the ruling tribe. It is in keeping with this thought that all through the Jewish age, Jesus was denominated the "Hope of Israel," and it is in keeping with the same truth that the coming of Jesus and His reign on the earth is set forth all through the New Testament, as "the Hope" of the Gentile believers. So the green rainbow and the emerald stone belong to Jesus in the special relationship of the King of the Jews, and the King of Saints, and the glorious rulership of this world in the millennial age. This color of green represents also the lifting of the curse from man and animals and the earth at the opening of the new age. If you will read the ninth chapter of Genesis and notice carefully you will see that the covenant which God made with Noah was a covenant first with Noah, and then with his children, and then with the cattle, and then with the fowls of the air, and then the creeping things, and then with the very earth itself, so that nothing was left out from the range of that covenant.

The same truth applies to the covenant which will be carried out in the theocratic government of Jesus on earth. The curse will be lifted from men, and women, and children, and from the four-footed beasts, and the fowls of the air, and the trees of the field, and the earth itself. The curse God put on man was that of hard work, and sweat; difficulty of making a living, and this will be lifted away. The curse God put on woman was that of suffering in her office as a mother in the bearing and caring for of children, and this curse will be removed at the opening of the millennial age from the people who are living at that time. Of course, we must remember that these truths apply, not to the glorified saints who have returned with Christ from the wedding, but to those human beings who have lived on the earth through the great tribulations, and who will be the progenitors of the millennial generations. The curse on the four-footed beasts was that of devouring each other, and this curse will be removed, for we are told emphatically that the lion will eat straw and grass, and be perfectly harmless in that age. The curse on the ground was that it should not bring forth its normal crops, and this curse will be removed under the reign of Jesus. "And all the trees will yield their fruit, and the earth will yield her increase," and one acre of ground will doubtless yield more than twenty acres now. The curse will be taken away from the atmosphere, and there will be no abnormal seasons, no storms, no cyclones, no earthquakes, but every movement of the four seasons, and of the winds, and the temperature, and of the harvests of the earth, will be as accurate, and beautiful, and harmonious, as the roll of the shining stars along their unvarying orbits. Everything will take on the character of verdure, and healthfulness, and vigor, and prosperity. All outward sin will be prohibited. Satan will be bound, and though the nations, by their natural generation, will have the principal of inward sin, the same as now, yet there will be no demons to tempt, and no outward forms of wickedness allowed, hence the people will be born under conditions of perfect love. Their intellects will be clear, and vigorous, and not possessed as they now are by demons. Everything will conduce to deep spirituality, and breadth, and clearness of intellectual wisdom, and the rapidly multiplying populations of that age will be under the continual guardianship, instruction, and dominion of the glorified saints, who will be, as Scripture teaches us, the elder brethren, that is "the church of the first born," to the nations who will live on the earth.

Thus the theocratic throne, with the emerald rainbow around it, sets forth the coming government, that it shall be one of glory and prosperity, extending from the centre of the throne out into all the ramified details of nature, and grace, and all men and animals, and the laws of the material world.

Chapter XVII
"THE LIVING CREATURES IN THE THRONE"
Rev. 4:6

AFTER TELLING US of the vision of the theocratic throne, with the Lord Jesus sitting on the throne, in the radiance of His glorified humanity, and the rainbow of emerald around the throne, the type of everlasting verdure and prosperity, both in the spiritual, and intellectual, and material world, the apostle proceeds to describe the "four living creatures" that sit with Christ in the midst of the throne, that is, the glorified members of His mystical body, who are to share with Him places of honor and authority in His everlasting government. The four and twenty elders referred to are doubtless the twelve patriarchs and the twelve apostles.

The four living creatures spoken of in this chapter are exactly the same as the living creatures described in Ezekiel's vision, and if we look carefully into the first and tenth chapters of Ezekiel, we find his vision a description of the opening of the millennial age, and the restoration of the Jews to their own land, under the restored throne of David, and the living creatures that moved like flashes of lightning, and had the appearance of burning coals of fire, that superintended the movement of the wheels, is a description of the ministry of the glorified saints in 1he millennial age.

Concerning these creatures, and their rank in the coming kingdom of Jesus, we may note the following items:

1. The four living creatures described by St. John and Ezekiel are identical with the beings elsewhere spoken of as the cherubim and seraphim. It is a great mistake to suppose that these beings are the same as those commonly called in Scripture the angels. All the names given to these cherubic living creatures are different from the names ascribed to the angels, and they are never used as synonyms with each other. Nor are the offices filled by these living creatures the same as the offices filled by the angels. Hence neither in their names, nor in their offices, nor in their ministry are they ever confounded with the angels. If the cherubim and seraphim, that is, these living creatures, had been representatives of angels, then their formation on the mercy seat would have been contrary to the commandment, which says, "Thou shalt not make any image of any creature in heaven above or earth beneath." But inasmuch as glorified humanity was not a fact at the time the law was given, the representation of them was only a prophecy of an order of creatures to come in the future age, and so the command was not violated.

2. Unless the cherubim represent redeemed and glorified humanity, then there was nothing in the whole system of Jewish typology to set it forth. In the structure of the Hebrew tabernacle and temple there was a careful representation of the whole process of redemption, of the incarnation of Jesus, of the atonement for sin, both ac-

tual and original, of repentance, of regeneration, of sanctification, and the gift of the Holy Spirit, all set forth in various forms and degrees. Now would it not be strange to set forth the whole purpose of redemption without having anything to represent the result of redemption, to emblematize the outcome of salvation in glorified humanity? Hence the erection of the cherubim on the mercy seat was a type of the living creatures that should be the outcome of redeeming grace and the glorified ministry of the coming age.

3. We learn from the writings of Moses that the form of the cherubim or the living creatures was made out of the identical same piece of gold that formed the lid of the mercy seat on the ark. They were not made of a separate piece of gold, or in any wise detached from the lid, but the same piece that formed the lid was turned up at the ends to form the image of the living creatures. This shows that the same piece of gold on which the blood was sprinkled was the identical one that formed the cherubim, illustrating that the same beings who were sprinkled by the precious blood of the atonement were to be the living creatures in whom should dwell the radiant fire of the shekinah, the living, burning presence of God Himself within them.

The word "cherub" means one who is "held fast," one seized upon as with a tight grasp, hence the cherubim was held fast to the lid of the mercy seat, and represents that thorough and perfect union between the Lord Jesus and those who are fully saved and established in holiness and held in His right hand, and who share the highest possible union with Christ in His life, and sufferings, and victory, and who are to have dominion.

The word "seraphim" means the '"burning ones, " those who are filled with the Holy Ghost and fire, typified by the shekinah flame that shone out between the wings of the cherubim over the ark. (Ps. 80. 1st).

4. These living creatures are set forth as being ministers of grace, which is nowhere the case with angels. One of these seraphims conveyed the live coal of fire to the lips of Isaiah, a type of the fire baptized ministry, conveying the living word of God to seeking souls, and rendering service in their purification. Also in the vision of Ezekiel these living creatures always go the way the Holy Spirit leads, and out of them went forth flashes of lightning, setting forth that they were the channels for the outflow of the Holy Spirit.

5. These living creatures are represented in the 5th chapter of Revelation as having the harps of God and golden vials full of odors, which are expressly said to be the prayers of the sanctified ones, and they sing the new song, praising the Lord Jesus who was slain and had redeemed them to God by His blood out of every kindred, and tongue, and people, and nation, and had made them unto God kings and priests, and they rejoiced that they should reign with Jesus on the earth. This proves absolutely and concisely everything I have said in the preceding items that they were redeemed and glorified men, and had been lifted to a place in the theocratic government of Jesus over the nations.

6. They arc called the four living creatures because "four" is that number which sets forth redeemed humanity, especially those who have very high rank among the redeemed and glorified ones. They had the face of a lion, typefying royalty, and the face of an ox, typefying humble service, the face of a man, signifying intelligence or enlightened reason, and the face of a soaring eagle, typefying supernatural and divine victory over all terrestrial things.

We have already seen the startling accuracy of analogy, between Noah and the flood, and the ark as representing the coming of Jesus, and the concurrent events. Now it was a singular providence, that God arranged that there should be just four men in the ark, and each man with his wife. These four men, coming forth from the ark at the opening of the new age, after the flood, was a perfect type of the four living creatures that John speaks of, as being in the throne with the Lord Jesus, at the opening of the millennial age. This is not all. During the days of Daniel in Babylon, Nebuchadnezzar fancied himself to be the fulfillment of that prophecy which told of one great God-man that should govern the whole world, and the great golden image which he set up was the picture of himself, as that great promised one who should rule the world. Now, singularly enough, God arranged to rebuke his impious blasphemy by setting forth a demonstration of the true Kingdom of God. The three Hebrew children were cast into the furnace of fire, and the great king looking in was astonished to find four men loose, walking in the flames, and one like unto the Son of God. There we have a perfect vision of Jesus as the God-man, with three of His chosen ones, making up the typical number of four, that should represent the coming Kingdom of God on earth. And we notice that Nebuchadnezzar issued at once a great proclamation concerning these four living ones that he saw in the furnace, "that God had shown signs and wonders concerning His Kingdom, which was an everlasting kingdom, and His dominion from generation to generation." Thus God rebuked the great monarch and revealed to him that the time was coming when God's Kingdom should fill this earth, and that it should be under the jurisdiction of glorified men that should be victorious, not only over all kings and despots, but over all the laws of nature and the power of fire.

Again we are told both by our Savior and by St. Peter that the transfiguration of Jesus was designed expressly to set forth "His coming and His kingdom." Now with the same accuracy of divine providence, Jesus took only three of the apostles with Him up into the mountain, and those the ones who lived in closest relationship with Himself, typefying the elected ones, or those who should be the most perfectly prepared. Jesus and Peter and James and John in that transfiguration glory correspond exactly with Noah and his three sons in the ark, and with the Son of God and the three Hebrews in the fiery furnace, and with the four living creatures in the millennial throne.

We must remember that the Scriptures represent Jesus as one with His saints, a brotherhood of kings. They are heirs and joint heirs to the same kingdom, and one of the amazing surprises that await the real humble followers of Jesus will be the extent to which they will share His joy, and glory, and honor, and dominion in His coming kingdom.

7. If we want to get a correct view of the mode of existence which will characterize the glorified saints during the millennial reign, we have it set forth in the manner of life which Jesus spent in the forty days after He arose from the dead. From the instant that Jesus arose from the dead, His body was glorified and absolutely free from all material laws, and under the supreme sway of the laws of the glorified world, if we can say that that state of being has any laws apart from the unlimited choice of the will. He told Mary when she approached Him near the sepulchre after He had arisen that He had not ascended to the Father. But that very day He did ascend to the Father and report the completed work of redemption, and that night showed Himself to His disciples, and invited them to handle Him and see that He was indeed the veritable Jesus of Nazareth. He appeared and disappeared at will, taking His body through stone walls, with barred doors, eating and drinking with His disciples, and communing with them familiarly and lovingly, and then vanishing out of their sight. Here we have the manner in which the glorified saints will live and reign with Christ during the millennial age. They are to be the priests, and

ministers, and teachers, and superintend all the details of life among the nations in that age, and, like the risen Jesus, will appear to the people on the earth to instruct, or aid, or correct, or commune with them at will, and at will vanish again into the air. The whole atmosphere surrounding the earth will be thronged day and night with these glorified ones, swiftly and safely moving hither and thither on the earth or in the air, singing as they go, with the harps of God in their hands, and crowns of gold upon their brow, and songs of ecstatic gladness on their lips, each one filling His own appointed mission in absolute harmony with each other and with their King.

It is very evident that all the millions of the other saved ones who did not rise in the first resurrection will be present with Jesus, and remain in their present state as disembodied and happy spirits awaiting them, as they do now, the general resurrection.

The apostle John tells us very definitely about the living creatures, and about the number that constitute the bride of the lamb being with Jesus in His throne, that is, rulers in His government, but he tells us of all the others of the saved ones from the earth, comprising a multitude that no man could number, that they stood before the throne, that is, they were members of the Kingdom of Heaven, and shared in its glory, but had not yet been raised to places of rulership in the kingdom. This is no fancy description of my own, but one that is expressly stated in several places and in different ways in the Word of God, and I must simply take the Word of God as it is. When the Scriptures speak of those persons who make up the bride of the Lamb, or who sit at the wedding supper, or who are rulers with Jesus, it always speaks of them as a definite number, but when the Scriptures speak of all the saved ones from the human race, including the saved among the heathen, who obeyed their light and the saved number of countless millions who have died in infancy, and the saved multitudes who are cleansed in the hour of death, it speaks of them as being like the sands of the seashore, and like the innumerable stars of heaven, and as being a multitude that no man could number. Hence the old notion that all the redeemed ones from the earth have the same rank in the future ages is utterly unscriptural as well as unreasonable. No one will reign with Jesus in His coming kingdom, except those who have paid for that privilege in this life by the humility and crucifixion of self and the testings of faith, which have qualified them for that position. This is exactly the teaching of Jesus when the mother of James and John requested that her two sons should sit the one on the right and the other on the left when He came to reign on this earth, and Jesus told her expressly that such positions in His coming kingdom had to be purchased by drinking His cup and sharing His baptism, and that no one could be lifted to such a principality in His empire, except those for whom it was prepared and those who were prepared for the position.

8. We are told in several places that these living creatures in the throne "are to rule the nations with a rod of iron," and that they "shall break all nations to pieces, as the vessels of the potter are broken to shivers," and "that they shall tread down the wicked as ashes under their feet," and that "they shall have dominion over the wicked."

Let us remember that at the opening of the millennial age, when Jesus and His saints return from the wedding, they will find the nations of the earth in a sad plight. Doubtless many will repent in the tribulations, but still sin will be rampant, and there will be a sharp, decisive conflict with ungodly men at the opening of the new age, to bring them into perfect subjection to the theocratic throne. This is strikingly declared and set forth in this 4th chapter by the words, that "out of the throne pro-

ceeded lightnings, and thunderings, and voices. " These
lightnings and thunderings are the imperial edicts that
will go forth among all nations at the very opening of the
millennial government. Many persons suppose that the
wicked nations on this earth are to be conquered by mild
and gradual processes of religion, but every place in Scripture which describes the conquering of the nations sets it
forth as a short, sharp, decisive conflict, not accomplished
by gospel principles, but by the imperial Son of God taking charge of the world and its people.

As soon as the throne of David is again set up in Jerusalem the myriads of glorified living creatures, members of
the bridehood of Christ, will go forth with princely power
into every nook and corner of the inhabitable globe. They
will search every house, and home, and building on earth,
and compel the inhabitants to burn up all whisky, and
intoxicants, and tobacco, and poisons, and bad pictures,
and erroneous books, and all the implements of war, or
cruelty, and all articles of art or furniture, which are the
works of the devil, or the instruments of sin, and the whole
world will be cleaned out in every department of indus-
try, commerce, or education, or social life, and the rod of
iron, or inflexible law of righteousness, will be put down
on every human being, and all the details of life. This is
the real meaning of that large class of Scriptures which
describe the dominion of saints, and ruling the nations
with a rod of iron.

Remember that these glorified beings will have power
equal to the angels, for Jesus says, those who shall be
counted, as the Greek has it, extra worthy of a place in
the first resurrection, shall be equal to the angels. The
look from an angel's face paralyzed the hundred soldiers
guarding the tomb of Jesus. The brush of an angel's wing
swept the breath out of 185,000 Assyrian soldiers slum-
ber-ing in their camp around Jerusalem in the days of
Hezekiah. Hence it will be impossible for the wicked to

resist the glorified saints when they come forth to revolutionize the world and reconstruct the whole human race on the basis of a divine government among men.

A very good illustration can be found in that of the conquest of England by William the Conqueror. Previous to his conquest, England was filled with petty kings and kingdoms, but the great William wiped out these petty kingdoms, and consolidated all England under one government, and he appointed his officers and soldiers, who had fought with him, to places in his kingdom, making them dukes, and earls, and lords, and knights, and assigning to them different counties and earldoms. And at the beginning of his consolidated government, he sent forth some thundering edicts among the people, and among them was an edict that the people of England should destroy every old wooden house, and build them houses of stone. This may serve to illustrate how Jesus the conqueror will wipe out all the national governments on this earth, and consolidate the entire human race under one government, with one language, and compel the people of the world to destroy their arts, and trades, and customs, and to adopt those new ones, which will be perfectly righteous, and humane, and equitable.

It is then that men will learn the art of war no more. The last vestige of it will pass away. There will be no more locks and keys, no more jails, or courthouses, or human legislatures, no more lawyers, or doctors, no more railroad magnates, or wheat gamblers, or scheming money lenders, or heretical teachings, or implements of vice, or games of chance, or theatres. Righteousness will fill the earth as the waters fill the sea. Everybody will be under the guardianship of the myriads of the glorified living creatures, and every department of life superintended by them, with inspired and infallible equity, and beauty, and gentle, tender love. The glorified ones will be the church of the first born, and they will take care of all the billions who will be born in that age, as a loving, thoughtful elder sister cares for the younger ones of the family.

9. After these revolutionary and reconstruction movements, typified by the lightnings and thunderings from the throne, John says he saw before the throne a sea of glass, clear as crystal. After the storm and shock of reconstruction has been gone through with, in which the nations of the world will make a rapid transition from anarchy to the heavenly theocracy, then the nations will be rapidly evangelized, and under the ministry of the glorified ones millions on millions will be speedily led to repentance, and saving faith, and sanctifying power. All demons will have been chained in the pit. People's consciences and minds will be open to truth. Their great sufferings will have conquered their pride. The blessed Holy Ghost will flood the world with His presence. The message of grace will be everywhere accompanied with divine power, and nations will be born to God in a day.

The words "sea" and "waters" in this book represent the souls of men. Clear, glassy water represents pure, sanctified souls. Hence, shortly after the throne of Jesus is set up, in front of the throne, the nations of the earth will be spread out, like a beautiful silver sea of transparent glass, their souls purified and filled with quietness, and love, and obedience, and all the moral, intellectual, and social conditions of mankind, will move onward through the bright, beautiful centuries, like a clear, glassy stream flowing smoothly over golden sands.

This same picture is given by John again in the 15th chapter, where he describes the glorified saints who had come off more than conquerors as standing on the glassy sea, that is, they presided over the tranquil, purified nations of the earth, and had the harps of God, and sung the song of Moses and the song of the Lamb.

There are times when we get very close to God, and His pure love burns so sweetly in our hearts that these visions given us by St. John are spread out so clearly before our eye of faith that we perceive them with a vividness and reality that make our heart flutter with the anticipation of the glory, and brightness, and sweetness, and music, and worship, and heavenly intelligence that will fill the world in those golden days. Who does not long to see these things come to pass? This is the vision that thrilled St. Paul when his head was on the chopping block, and he saw that crown of righteousness that he would wear in Christ's coming kingdom, and saw other crowns for all those who love the appearing and coming reign of the Lord Jesus.

When King Solomon built the temple he put in front of the altar a brazen sea supported by twelve brazen oxen. This was an inspired type. Solomon's reign was a type of the millennial kingdom, and the brazen sea a type of the sea of glass, or sanctified society, and being supported by twelve oxen, typefied that the millennial kingdom would be supported by the members of Christ's bridehood, that is, the twelve times twelve of the hundred and forty-four thousand. Well may we say, "blessed and holy are they that shall have a part in the first resurrection, and that shall be counted worthy of a place to reign with Jesus in His throne and in His kingdom."

Conclusion

I HAVE NOT HAD SPACE in this book to give a detailed account of the many prophecies which refer to the millennial age, or to set before the reader the marvelous glories that will fill the earth at that time in the extraordinary inventions, and the social, intellectual, and spiritual progress that will then be developed.

We learn from several prophecies such as "The child shall die a hundred years old, and the age of my people shall be as the age of a tree," that human life among those who are born in that age will be lengthened to antediluvian lifetime. We must remember, however, that the human race will still be in a fallen condition, and those who are born in that age will have the principle of original sin in their nature, hence the Scriptures do not teach that everybody born in that age will be holy. Several places in the Book of Psalms, it is said in the margin, that many people in that time "will serve the King feignedly." Hence toward the close of that age there will be great multitudes who have secret sin in their hearts, and will be open to the delusion and devices of a tempting devil. So John tells us "that after the thousand years are ended Satan will again be loosed out of his prison for a short time, and go forth to deceive these multitudes" who harbor inward sin, and they will rebel against the dominion of the saints; then lightning from heaven will destroy every one of them. Then follows the general resurrection, of both great and small, all the dead who had not been raised in the first resurrection. Then the great white throne is set up in the regions of the air, and every human being will be assembled, and stand one by one before that throne to give an account of himself. This great judgment day may last a thousand years, or a sufficient time for all the untold millions of earth to render an exact detail account of his life during probation.

During that time the earth will be burned over, and crystalized into a glorious orb, and the water in the sea will be consumed by the fire, and the whole planet celestialized, and made a part of the heaven of glory. The lost will be banished into the outer regions of darkness, and the saved of all the ages, both "the church of the first born," and the church of the second born, and the myriads that were saved in the millennial age, will return to the glorified earth as their home, with the privileges of angels and glorified beings of other worlds, of moving to and fro throughout all the whole universe according to the will of God.

There are intimations in Scripture that all the created worlds will be in the future ages filled with intelligent populations, and that God will use the saved and glorified millions of this earth as missionaries and ministers to the younger races of beings on the other worlds to warn them against falling into sin by rehearsing to them the awful history of sin in our own world.

St. Paul says in the close of his wonderful prayer in Ephesians that God will glorify Himself in the church unto the generations of the ages of ages, and by some inexcusable blunder in our common version of the Bible the word "generations" in the Greek is entirely left out in our translation. And John tells us that after the new heavens and the new earth in the glorified state we shall serve the Lord our God for ever and ever.

Supplement Chapter
CHRIST'S RETURN TO JERUSALEM

WHEN WE HAVE a clear spiritual apprehension of the coming of Christ back to this earth to gather out His saints and glorify them, and then to assume personal dominion over the nations of the earth for a thousand years, it enables us to understand a great multitude of Scripture passages which are otherwise enveloped in great mist, or else entirely unintelligible. There are many acts in the life of Jesus which seem without significance, unless interpreted as prophetic events to be accomplished in His return back to this earth. There are many things recorded in the gospels that never have had their proper weight with believers, and are seen only as brilliant fragments in the life of Jesus, because they have not been looked upon in the light of His premillennial coming, and as prophetic events of His reign on the earth. The banquet at Bethany is declared by Christ Himself as prophetic, and when Mary anointed Him with spikenard as being a prophecy of His death and burial, and the breaking of the alabaster box, the breaking of His body, and pouring forth the ointment, the pouring forth of His life on the world. The transfiguration was given expressly as a prophetic sample of His second coming and outshining of His glory when He gathers His elect ones from heaven and earth up into the air; and there is no proper understanding of that event except as a type of His second coming. In like manner the account of Jesus riding into Jerusalem as recorded in the 21st of Matthew can have no adequate interpretation except as a prophetic event of His return to this earth. Let us turn to the 21st of Matt, and study the event recorded from the first to the sixteenth verse in the light of Christ's return, and we will see that instead of its being a mere transient act in the earthly life of Christ, it stretches away across the centuries, and assumes the magnitude of a glorious and worldwide fulfillment in the coming kingdom of our Lord.

First. We see in this account that our Lord was returning to Jerusalem for the last time from the east side of Jordan. He came up by Jericho, where He healed the blind man, and as He approached the vicinity of Jerusalem He providentially allowed the people to make great demonstrations, and He Himself seemed about to assume the throne of David. This was a prophetic act of the time when He shall return from the wedding and come back to Jerusalem in the capacity of the King of kings and Lord of lords, to set up His throne over the nations of the earth. In His parables, Jesus represents Himself as being now in a far country, and having a kingdom prepared for Him, and that all His true servants are being put to a test in regard to their heart loyalty and their individual stewardship of His gifts and grace.

But just as certainly as this nobleman has called His servants, and given them various gifts and responsibilities, and is now gone into a far country, so certainly will He return to the very city, and country, and earth, from whence He went.

Second. We see in this account of the triumphal entry of Jesus into Jerusalem, that He laid aside His usual conduct of being a servant, and began to assume the conduct of authority, and royalty, and to exercise that legitimate authority which belonged to Him as an inherent king over His subjects. He sent two of His disciples into the village, and commanded them to take the young ass and colt, on which no man had ever rode, and to bring it to Him, and said, "If any man shall say ought to you about it, you shall say, 'The Lord hath need of him.'" This incident rises out from the usual tenor of the life of Jesus, as an abrupt mountain rises from a plain, and it is marked all over with the character of absolute ownership and authority over all men and animals. Jesus was the absolute proprietor of those disciples, and of that colt, and of the man who temporarily owned the colt, as He was the proprietor of every atom on the earth, and of all worlds, and of all creatures. But all through His life He acted as one utterly poor, and forewent all His rights as a God and a king, depending on others for His sustenance, and living as a beneficiary on the charity of His creatures. But in this event, the veil of absolute poverty is, for a moment, rent asunder, and He emerges from His life of poverty, and His words and actions betray Him to be absolute owner of all things. We never can understand this act in its vast magnitude until we make it the telescope through which we look over the centuries to the time when He shall again return to Jerusalem, no longer in the guise of a servant, and depending on His creatures, but as Lord and monarch over everybody and everything, whether angels, or men, or animals, or the inanimate creation. And when looked at in this light, how this simple record in Matthew towers aloft, and expands into a vast and broad significance, which gives it a meaning equal to the glorious personage of the Lord Jesus.

Third. We are told in these verses, that Jesus entered Jerusalem in the capacity of a king. "All this was done that it might be fulfilled which was spoken of the prophet, saying, 'Tell you the daughter of Sion, behold, thy king cometh unto thee.'" I want to ask, in all seriousness, that if this event was not arranged as a prophecy of Christ's return to Jerusalem, to govern the earth, then where might be its real meaning? Jesus had lived on the earth about 33 years, and up to this time He had never assumed any real kingly prerogatives, nor exercised any authority over His creatures except as a spiritual teacher, and yet it is expressly said He was born to be a king over men, and over this earth, and no mythical king over an empire of Swedenborgian mysticism, but a *bona fide* king over real men. And now He for a few brief hours only, gives forth a manifestation of Himself in a kingly capacity, and then the brief pageant of one quickly-flying day passes out of sight; this great king sinks back into the old role of poverty and persecution, and the shadows of a disgraceful death. Let us turn to the prophecy referred to by Matthew, in Isaiah 62:11: "Behold, the Lord hath proclaimed unto the end of the world; say ye to the daughter of Zion, behold, thy salvation cometh." Also to Zech. 9:9, "Rejoice greatly, oh, daughter of Zion; shout, oh, daughter of Jerusalem; behold, thy king cometh unto thee, who is just, and having salvation; lowly, and riding upon an ass, and upon a colt the foal of an ass. And I will cut off the chariot from Ephraim, and the horse from Jerusalem, and the battle bow shall be cut off, and He shall speak peace unto the heathen, and His dominion shall be from sea to sea, and from the river to the ends of the earth.

Now in the light of this prophecy it is simply preposterous absurdity to say that all this magnificent prophecy by Zechariah was fulfilled in that one transient demonstration of Jesus entering Jerusalem, which filled less than one day with an exhibition of His royalty. When we compare the huge dimensions of Zechariah's prophecy with this account of Christ's triumphal entry into Jerusalem we see plainly that that entry was a brief, dazzling, prophetic event of the time when the prophecy should be accomplished. The prophet tells us in connection with Christ's riding into Jerusalem that there will be a doing away of war chariots and of war horses, and the destruction of the battle bow, and that it will be a time when God shall speak peace among all heathen, and the vestiges of war will pass away, and the time when the dominion of this king of Zion shall stretch from sea to sea, and from the river to the ends of the earth. This prophecy does not refer to the third heavens, and where the Father now has His throne, nor to some ethereal mystical heaven which floats in common church theology, but emphatically to this earth and to the heathen nations on this earth, and to the literal city of Jerusalem, and to Jesus being the literal king over the sea and over the earth. We know that that prophecy was not fulfilled in that momentary pageant when Christ rode into Jerusalem, and it never has yet been fulfilled, for the heathen do not have peace, and wars still exist. But when we look at that event as prophetic of Jesus returning to this earth, and to Jerusalem, riding in majesty on His own creatures as absolute proprietor and king over all men, and animals, and sea, and land, then it becomes perfectly intelligible, and has an import which makes it equal to all the character and conduct of Jesus.

Fourth. When Christ went riding into the city there were two companies, one went with Him and the other came out from the city to meet Him. And so we read that one multitude went before Him, and another followed Him, and they cried, saying: "Hosannah to the

Son of David." This was prophetic of the two companies that will greet the Lord Jesus, and hail Him as
king of the world. One company will descend with
Him from the wedding. Those saints who are counted
worthy to be raised in the first resurrection, and those
who shall be prepared to be caught away at His appearing; these will be glorified and be with Him at the
banquet in the air, and these are the ones who will
return from the wedding. And then as He descends in
fulfillment of prophecy to put His foot again on Mt.
Olivet, the people on the earth who will have passed
through the great tribulations will have been sufficiently humbled to hail Him as their king, and especially will this be true of the twelve tribes of Israel,
who at that time will recognize Him as their Messiah,
and will gladly shout hosannahs to Him as the Son of
David and as their Lord and King. Thus the multitude
that has been glorified with Him and the multitude
that has been subdued by the great tribulations will
both unite in shouting His praises and rending the air
with the melodies and thunder and of their applause
as He returns to Jerusalem to set up His theocratic
kingdom over all the earth.

Fifth. We see that both of these multitudes in their
hosannahs said, expressly, "Jesus is the Son of David."
Jesus is not only God, but a man, and, in His humanity,
the offspring of King David, who was the founder of the
theocracy, and Jesus as Son of David is the direct lineal
heir to the throne of David. Now it is significant that since
the birth of Jesus the Jews have never been able to find
the rightful undeparted heir to the throne of David, for
the lines of pedigree from the birth of Jesus ran off into so
many directions it has been impossible for them to fix on
the lineage of the true heir, and the man Jesus, the son of
Mary, stands forth in history as the last and only heir to
the theocratic throne which was established by David,

the man after God's own heart. For nearly two thousand years the Jewish throne has been in eclipse, but the day is fast approaching when Jesus as David shall descend to this earth and triumphantly ride into Jerusalem and assume command over the twelve tribes of Israel and all the nations of the earth. This is eminently the prophecy in the third chapter of Hosea. "For the children of Israel shall abide many days without a king and without a prince and without a sacrifice, and afterwards shall the children of Israel return and seek the Lord their God, and David their king, and shall fear the Lord and His goodness in the latter days." Here Jesus is definitely spoken of as the Lord and as David, and as ruling on this earth over the twelve tribes in the later days, that is, in the last age, which is the millennial age.

Sixth. When Christ went riding into the city, accompanied by these shouting multitudes, we are told that all the city was moved at the spectacle, saying, "Who is this?" And the multitude said, "This is Jesus." This item will be most perfectly fulfilled when Jesus returns to set up His government. All the people on the earth who have survived the great tribulations will be profoundly moved to the innermost depths of their being in that memorable day. Let us remember at that time the hundreds of millions on the earth will be in an unsaved condition, rent and torn by the storms of the great tribulation, but ignorant of God and of salvation, and the nations of the earth will just be emerging from a state of anarchy, so that when Christ and the glorified saints return to the earth it may well strike a supernatural awe into all other spirits.

Let us notice the striking contrast between the multitudes who followed Jesus into the city and the people of the city who were so moved at the spectacle. Those who followed Him were filled with enthusiastic praises, casting their garments in the way, they prostrated themselves along the road, their very souls bursting forth with enthusiastic applause. That scene faintly indicates the unbounded adoration and worship that will be given to Jesus by those who accompany Him back to this earth; they will throng His descending pathway from the heavenly wedding, and throw themselves millions on millions in postures of adoration and love and praise before Him, casting their crowns at His feet, and rending the very skies with their sweet voiced hallelujahs.

I may stop here to say that those persons who will be among that happy throng are those who already in this life have abandoned themselves utterly to Jesus, and often prostrated themselves in humble secret prayer, casting their words and thoughts and lives like green boughs under His blessed feet, and receive Him already as their absolute owner and king in all the affairs of life. But those people who were in the city, and who were excited and moved at the royal procession, represent the unsaved nations on the earth when Jesus comes with His glorified army to take possession.

Seventh. After reaching the temple Jesus dismounted from the colt, and went into the temple of God and cast out all them that bought and sold their merchandise, and overthrew the tables of money changers and the seats of them that sold doves. This act of supreme authority in the temple of God of purging the temple of the money changers is in perfect keeping with His whole conduct as a king on that occasion, and is prophetic of that complete purging of the holy temple, and of all the things of this earth, when He establishes His reign over the world. We are told in the third chapter of Jeremiah "that at that time Jerusalem will be the throne of the Lord," and we are told in many prophecies that Jesus shall reign in Sion, and in Jerusalem, and on the throne of David, and at that time He will purge Jerusalem. Thus when we look at this act at the close of that eventful day of purging the temple, it is a prophetic event of the earth-cleansing which Jesus will exercise at the opening of His millennial reign, it has a magnitude of meaning which this Scripture could never have, except as viewed in this light. It is also significant that immediately following this austere purging of the temple, which had been made a den of thieves, there flocked around Him the blind and the lame in multitudes, and He healed them all.

What act in the life of Jesus could more beautifully set forth the character of the beginning of His millennial reign. At that time He will most thoroughly upset all the ungodly practices on the earth, and destroy every form of unrighteous traffic among the nations; but this very austerity of royal power will draw to Him the suffering, and the afflicted, and the weary-hearted ones, who have gone through the awful storm of the tribulation; and, right in connection with the suppressing of all wickedness among the nations, Jesus will exercise infinite compassion in healing all the sick on the earth, and comfort the broken-hearted, and extend His saving grace to all nations, and so work through the agency of His glorified saints, and the omnipresent power of the Holy Ghost, that in a short time from the setting up of His throne in Jerusalem, the earth shall be filled with the glory of God, as the waters fill the sea. Thus we discover that this brilliant pageant of Christ entering Jerusalem, was not merely for that one day, but, like a momentary sign in the roll of history, it furnishes a brief sample of what will occur again— not as a transient event of a day, but as an abiding and world-wide fulfillment and of a magnitude that shall comport with Him as Lord of lords and King of kings!